FODOR'S

SWEDEN
1988

Area Editor: Philip Ray
Editorial Contributors: Andrew Brown, Robert Brown
Editor: Thomas Cussans
Executive Editor: Richard Moore
Illustrations: Elizabeth Haines
Maps: Swanston Graphics

FODOR'S TRAVEL PUBLICATIONS, INC.
New York and London

ISBN 0-679-01568-X
ISBN 0-340-41804-4 (Hodder & Stoughton)

Parts of FODOR'S SWEDEN have been excerpted from FODOR'S SCANDINAVIA 1988.

MANUFACTURED IN THE UNITED STATES OF AMERICA
10 9 8 7 6 5 4 3 2 1

CONTENTS

FOREWORD

All in all, it's hard to think of reasons *not* to go to Sweden. True, it can be expensive, and those on a budget may find themselves wanting to limit their time in Stockholm, the country's incomparably beautiful capital city. But then again, Stockholm aside, the particular pleasures of Sweden are nearly all to be found in the great outdoors. Unpopulated forests, spangled by clear, ice-blue rivers and lakes, and unspoiled countryside stretch almost the entire length of the country, from the Kattegat in the south to the empty tracts of the Artic Circle in the far north. The opportunities for openair holidays—farm vacations (raised to a fine art here), riding, camping, fishing, sailing, canoeing, skiing, and so on—are second to none. Moreover, the very industriousness that has raised Sweden to her present lofty place on the world's pecking order ensure that these activities are both excellently organized·*and* extremely good value for money.

There are other plus marks too. Sweden is easy to reach and easy to travel around. The quality of hotels, even those in the depths of the country, is almost always high. There are a whole host of travel bargains, museum entry cards and inexpensive hotel and restaurant deals. And there is the added bonus of knowing that English will not only be spoken, it will be spoken excellently.

* * * *

While every care has been taken to insure the accuracy of the information contained in this guide, the publishers cannot accept responsibility for any errors that may appear.

All prices quoted in this guide are based on those available to us at the time of writing. In a world of rapid change, however, the possibility of inaccurate or out-of-date information can never be totally eliminated. We trust therefore, that you will take prices quoted as indicators only, and will double-check to be sure of the latest figures.

Similarly, be sure to check all opening times of museums and galleries. We have found that such times are liable to change without notice, and you could easily make a trip only to find a locked door.

When a hotel closes or a restaurant produces a disappointing meal, let us know, and we will investigate the establishment and the complaint. We are always ready to revise our entries for the following year's edition should the facts warrant it.

Send your letters to the editors of Fodor's Travel Publications, 201 E. 50th Street, New York, NY 10022. European readers may prefer to write to Fodor's Travel Guides, 9-10 Market Place, London W1N 7AG, England.

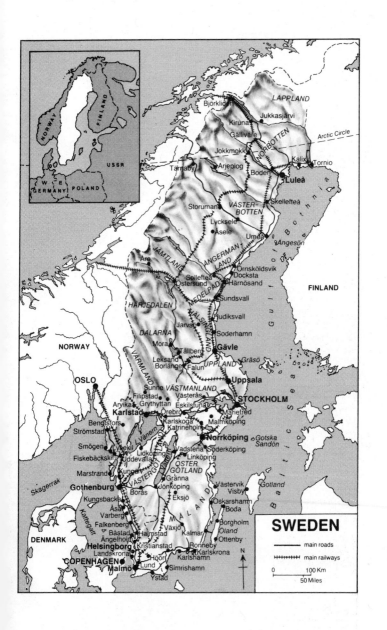

SWEDEN

FACTS AT YOUR FINGERTIPS

Planning Your Trip

 NATIONAL TOURIST OFFICE. In the U.S.: Swedish Tourist Board, 655 Third Ave., New York, NY 10017 (212–949–2333).

In the U.K.: Swedish National Tourist Office, 3 Cork St., London W.1 (01–437 5816).

Within Sweden, there are around 380 local tourist offices, about 180 of which are open all year round. Lists are available from the Swedish Tourist Board, but we also give addresses and telephone numbers of all the major tourist offices at the beginning of each *Practical Information* section. Local tourist offices are usually located in the center of towns and can be identified by a green "i" symbol.

 WHEN TO GO. By far and away the best time to visit Sweden is in the summer. The Swedish winter is not only very long and very cold, with short days, but almost all the major tourist facilities—museums, sightseeing excursions, ferries, even many museums—are scaled right down or in some cases, closed completely. More to the point, however, is the fact that most of the real fun to be had in Sweden takes place outdoors, and with the exception of winter sports there is very little you are liable to want to do, or will even be able to do, outside during the Swedish winter. That said, however, clear, crisp and sunny days are by no means uncommon in the winter, and though short they can be delightful.

Nonetheless, it is from mid-May to mid-September that Sweden is at its best. Summer temperatures are surprisingly high—certainly comparable to Maine or Vermont, for example—while the sea is generally much warmer than you might expect, largely as a result of the shallowness of the Baltic. You may consider visiting in April or late September, but bear in mind that the weather can be unpredictable.

Sweden has well-developed winter resorts, offering cross-country skiing, skating and curling, though little in the way of Alpine, or downhill, skiing.

 SEASONAL EVENTS. Summer sees the bulk of Sweden's seasonal events and the Swedish Tourist Board and local tourist offices will be able to advise what's happening where. But the following are some of the major events.

February has the Great Lapp Winter Fair in Jokkmokk in the far north of Sweden.

March sees a more modern winter event, the 55-mile cross-country ski race from Sälen to Mora; over 10,000 people take part.

April sees a major horse show at the Scandinavium, Gothenburg.

April 30 is Walpurgis Night, when the end of the winter is celebrated; fires are lit throughout the country.

June 6 is Swedish National Day, with celebrations the length and breadth of the country. Stockholm's Skansen Park is the site of the most dramatic festivities. Midsummer Day is celebrated with equal gusto, especially in the provinces of Dalarna and Hälsingland.

July sees the Visby Festival, held in the ruins of the medieval cathedral there. The Swedish Derby is also held now, at Jägersro in Malmö.

August has a series of Swedish-American days, notably at Skansen Park in Stockholm and at Växjö in southern Sweden.

September—the International Consumer Goods Fair at Gothenburg, incorporating the "Household of Today" exhibition.

December has many events celebrating the imminent arrival of Christmas, notably St. Lucia's Day on the 13th, celebrated throughout Sweden (you'll also find a picture of St. Lucia in every hotel). The Nobel Prize awards take place in December in Stockholm (by invitation only).

National Holidays. Jan. 1 (New Year's Day); Jan. 6 (Epiphany); Apr. 1–4 (Easter); May 12 (Ascension); May 23 (Whit Mon.); June 25 (Midsummer); Nov. 5 (All Saints); Dec. 26 (Boxing Day).

WHAT TO PACK. The golden rule is to travel light; generally, try not to take more than you can carry yourself. Not only are porters more or less wholly extinct in Europe these days (where you can find them they're very expensive anyway), the less luggage you take the easier checking in and out of hotels becomes, similarly airports (increasingly the number one nightmare of all modern travel) become much easier to get through and, if you only take one piece of luggage, the less risk there is of your luggage being lost en route, and, in theory anyway, the less time you need to wait for it to appear when you get off the plane. It's an excellent idea also to make sure that your luggage is sturdy; there's no worse way to start or finish your vacation than by discovering that your clothes are generously distributing themselves along a station platform or, even worse, have already scattered themselves around the hold of a 747. It can also be a good idea to pack the bulk of your things in one large bag and put everything you need for overnight, or for two or three nights, in a smaller one, to obviate packing and repacking at brief stops.

Bear in mind that on trans-Atlantic flights there is, in any case, a size limit to the amount of luggage you may take with you. Charges for excess baggage are high. On most flights you may check in no more than two pieces of luggage, neither more than 62 inches overall (that is, height plus length plus width) and both together no more than 106 inches. Hand baggage is restricted to one piece no more than 65 inches overall.

Having said all this, however, don't forget to leave room for shopping. Though at the same time remember that almost all Swedish stores can have goods sent directly to your home.

Clothes. Informality is the key word throughout Sweden. So at even the smartest restaurants or at the theater—and this applies to the opera and ballet as well—you are not likely to have to dress up. Those few restaurants that do expect men to wear a tie will always lend you one if necessary. Thus normal summer clothes, with a generous sprinkling of sports clothes, will happily suffice, but also take along sweaters and stout shoes if you are going into the mountains. And don't forget a light topcoat or raincoat. The summer weather is generally fine, but rain is by no means uncommon. If you are going to Sweden in the winter, it will be very cold, so take along plenty of warm clothing. Be prepared to shed it once indoors, however; Swedish central heating is nothing if not efficient.

Finally, mosquitoes, especially in the far north, can be a real nuisance from the end of June to early August. Take some repellent with you.

TAKING MONEY ABROAD. Traveler's checks are still the standard and best way to safeguard your travel funds; and you will usually get a better exchange rate in Europe for traveler's checks than for cash. In the U.S., Bank of America and Republic Bank of Dallas issue checks only in U.S. dollars; Thomas Cook issues checks in U.S., British and Australian currencies; Barclays Bank in dollars and pounds; and American Express in U.S., Canadian, French, German, British, Swiss and Japanese currencies. Your choice of branch will depend on several factors. American Express checks are widely known, Bank of America has some 28,000 correspondents throughout the world, Thomas Cook about 20,000. The best-known British checks are Cook's and those of Barclays, Lloyds, Midland and National Westminster banks.

Britons holding a Uniform Eurocheque card and cheque book—apply for them at your bank—can cash cheques for up to £100 a day at banks participating in the scheme and write cheques for goods and services—in hotels, restaurants, shops, etc.—again up to £100.

Credit Cards. Most major credit cards are generally, but by no means universally, accepted in larger Swedish hotels, restaurants and shops. Accordingly, you would be well advised to check carefully which cards *are* accepted, particularly in hotels and restaurants, before checking in or ordering a meal.

Our hotel and restaurant listings in the *Practical Information* sections at the end of every chapter give details of each of the four major cards—American Express, Diner's Club, MasterCard (incorporating Access and EuroCard) and Visa, which are listed under the abbreviations AE, DC, MC and V—accepted in each hotel and restaurant we carry. But as we say, double check. As a general rule, you will find that Visa is the most commonly accepted.

 CURRENCY. The unit of currency in Sweden is the *krona* (plural, *kronor*), or crown. It is divided into 100 öre and written as SEK. There are coins (all silver) of 10 and 50 öre and of 1 and 5 SEK; notes come in denominations of 10, 50, 100, 500 and 10,000 SEK. The rate of exchange at the time of writing (mid-1987) was 6.32 SEK to the U.S. dollar and 10.30 SEK to the pound sterling. However, these rates will certainly change both before and during 1988, so check them carefully when planning your trip and on it.

You can change money or traveler's checks in banks, exchange offices and many post offices. Some hotels will also change money for you, but their rate is likely to be much less favorable.

 COSTS IN SWEDEN. Sweden is a country with a high standard of living and many costs are correspondingly high. Some items—liquor especially, particularly the imported variety—are very expensive, while most are perhaps no more than 10–15% more expensive than their equivalents in the U.S.

However, a relatively low rate of inflation, estimated at only 3% for 1987, plus vigorous efforts by the Swedes, who are only too conscious of their high-pricetag reputation, mean that for most visitors it should be possible to keep most expenses within reasonable bounds. Many hotels for example have special low summer rates and also cut costs during weekends in winter. Many restaurants offer, throughout the year, a low-cost menu at an all-in-one price for a special dish of the day, salad, light beer or milk, bread and butter and coffee. There are likewise many discounts available for train, plane and bus travel, and most larger cities also have inexpensive tourist cards giving free travel on public transport and free entry into many museums. We give details of all these schemes in the sections that follow. The Swedish Tourist Board also has full details; alternatively, ask your travel agent.

Sample costs. A cinema seat for one, SEK 40; visit to a museum, SEK 10; coffee, SEK 7; glass of beer, SEK 9–35 depending on strength; bottle of wine, SEK 70–110; Coke, SEK 8; a moderate taxi ride, SEK 38; an average bus or subway ride, SEK 8.

LANGUAGE. The Swedes are great linguists. Most speak excellent English, and a good number also manage more than just a smattering of French and German. Most films and many TV programs are also in English with Swedish subtitles.

TIME. Sweden is one-hour ahead of Greenwich Mean Time and six hours ahead of Eastern Standard Time (seven hours ahead during summer).

Getting to Sweden

FROM THE U.S. BY AIR. Flights from major departure points in the U.S. and Canada to the Swedish capital, and some other major Swedish cities, are reasonably frequent and generally easy to arrange. And, given the perpetual battle for customers among airlines flying the Atlantic, even to relatively less important destinations such as Sweden, fares are generally inexpensive.

However, be warned that though fares may be low and flights numerous, long-distance flying today is no bed of roses. Lines and delays at ever-more crowded airports, perfunctory in-flight service and shrinking leg-room on board a giant jet with some 400 other people, followed by interminable waits for your luggage when you arrive, are the clearest possible signals that the glamor of air travel—if it ever existed—is very much a thing of the past.

Unfortunately, these problems are compounded when flying to Europe by the fact that most flights from the States are scheduled to arrive first thing in the morning. Not only are you in for a night's discomfort on the plane, but you arrive at the start of a new day to be greeted by the confusion (some would say chaos) of a modern airport. To make life even more difficult for the weary traveler, many hotels will not allow you to check in before noon or even 1 P.M. giving you as much as six hours with nothing to do and nowhere to go.

There are a number of steps you can take, however, in order to lessen the traumas of long-distance flying. The first and possibly most important of all is to harbor no illusions about the supposed luxury. If you approach your flight knowing that you are going to be cooped up for a long time and will have to face delays and discomforts of all kinds, the odds are that you will get through it without doing terrible things to your blood pressure or being disillusioned—but there's no point expecting comfort, good service and efficiency because you won't get them.

The right attitude is half the battle, but there are a number of other practical points to follow. Wear comfortable, loose-fitting clothes and take off your shoes. Try to sleep as much as possible, especially on night flights; this can very often mean not watching the movie (they are invariably dull anyway) as it will probably be shown during the only period when meals are not being served and you can sleep. If you have difficulty sleeping, or think you might, take along a light sedative and try to get a window seat in order to avoid being woken up to let the person next to you get to the toilet or being bashed by people walking down the aisle. Above all, avoid alcohol, or at least drink only a little. The dry air of a pressurized airplane causes rapid dehydration, exaggerating the effects of drink and jet lag. Similarly, drink as much water as possible. Finally, once you arrive, try to take things easily for a day or so. In the excitement of being in a new place, especially for the first time, you can very often not realize how tired you are and optimistically set out sightseeing, only to come down to earth with a bump. Whatever you do, don't have any business meetings for at least 24 hours after arriving.

Fares. With air fares in a constant state of flux, the best advice for anyone planning to fly to Sweden independently (rather than as part of a package tour, in which case your flight will have been arranged for you) is to check with a travel agent and let him make your reservations for you. Nonetheless, there are a number of points to bear in mind.

The best bet is to buy either an Apex or Super Apex ticket. First Class, Business and even the misleadingly-named Economy, though giving maximum flexibility on flying dates and cancellations, as well as permitting stopovers, are extremely expensive. Apex and Super Apex, by contrast, are reasonably priced and offer the all-important security of fixed return dates (all Apex tickets are round trip). In addition, you get exactly the same service as flying Economy. However, there are a number of restrictions: you must book, and pay for, your ticket 21 days or more in advance; you can stay in Sweden no less than and no longer than a stated period (usually six days and six months); if you miss your flight, you forfeit the fare. But from the point of view of price and convenience, these tickets certainly represent the best value for money.

If your plans are sufficiently flexible and tighter budgeting is important, you can sometimes benefit from the last-minute bargains offered by tour operators otherwise unable to fill their plane or quota of seats. A number of brokers specializing in these discount sales have sprung up who can book seats of this type. All charge an annual membership fee, usually around $35–45.

Among them are: *Stand-Buys Ltd.,* 311 West Superior, Ste. 414, Chicago, IL 60610 (312–943–5737); *Moments Notice,* 40 East 49th St., New York, NY 10017 (212–486–0503); *Discount Travel Intl.,* 114 Forest Ave., Narberth, PA 19072 (215–668–2182); and *Worldwide Discount Travel Club,* 1674 Meridian Ave., Miami Beach, FL 33139 (305–534–2082).

Charter flights are also available to Sweden, though their number has decreased in recent years. Again, a travel agent will be able to recommend the most reliable. You might also consider, though this too should be done via a travel agent, buying a package tour to Sweden but using only the plane ticket. As packagers are able to get substantial discounts on fares through block booking seats, the price of the total package can sometimes be less than an ordinary air fare alone.

 FROM THE U.K. BY AIR. Stockholm is well served by regular flights from the U.K., principally from London's Heathrow and Gatwick airports, but there are also flights from a limited number of other U.K. airports. There are at least four flights a day to Stockholm.

Fares. European air fares are high, disproportionately so in many cases, and unfortunately flights to Sweden are no exception.

Accordingly, it is well worth searching out the bucket shop ads in the Sunday papers and magazines such as *Time Out* and *Business Traveler* (the latter an excellent source of information on budget fares). Bucket shops—some more reliable than others, so don't hand over all your money until you have the ticket—offer tickets at rates significantly below the so-called official ones, and can often prove very good value. But they do often operate at rather short notice and so may not be suitable for anyone hoping to book their flight some time in advance.

 FROM THE U.K. BY TRAIN. If you are in a hurry, go by air! The Scandinavian countries, with the exception of Denmark, are relatively isolated from the U.K. and the rail/ferry trek can occupy up to two full days. The approximate journey time to Stockholm is 31 hours.

This having been said, getting to Sweden by train and ferry is great fun. The classic route is from London (Liverpool Street) to Harwich by rail, then by ferry to the Hook of Holland. From the Hook of Holland you go by train on to Hamburg, then by way of the Vogelfluglinie and the Puttgarden to Rødby train ferry to the Danish capital, Copenhagen. From Copenhagen the routes fan out to the other Nordic countries.

The "Nord West Express" is a useful service, with a morning departure (day 1) from London, giving a daytime crossing of the North Sea to Holland. The main train leaves the Hook at 8 in the evening and then runs overnight to arrive in Copenhagen just after 8 the following morning (day 2). Second-class couchettes are available from the Hook to Copenhagen and there are also ordinary seats. Alternatively use the "Holland-Scandinavia Express." This departs from London (Liverpool Street) in the evening (7.50) and the North Sea crossing is made overnight. Departure from the Hook is at 7.10 A.M. on day 2 and Copenhagen is reached at 7.10 P.M. The great advantage of this service is that it gives you a more comfortable overnight crossing on the ferry. You also travel over the beautiful Vogelfluglinie with its spectacular Fehmarn bridge and enjoy the Puttgarden to Rødby crossing all in daylight. One note: at Puttgarden the whole train goes on board the ship so there's no need to change.

There are also other rail routes to Copenhagen involving much shorter train journeys if you don't like the idea of the long overland haul. *DFDS* ferries for example operate from Harwich and Newcastle to Esbjerg in Jutland. For real comfort and personal service try their *Commodore Class* cabins. (There are connecting rail services from London to Harwich and from Esbjerg to Copenhagen by the aptly named "Englanderen.") On this route, by leaving London in the early afternoon of day 1 you will be in Copenhagen at 7.00 P.M. the following day. It is essential to book seats on this train, in either direction: Dkr. 10 booking fee on top of fare (this is sometimes cheaper mid-week, always worth checking at station booking offices). Overnight crossings can also be made on the *Fred Olsen Line* from Harwich to Hirtshals in Jutland, which is a stop-over on the Harwich–Oslo route.

Alternatively, if you wish to minimize the sea crossing make use of the Jetfoil service *(Thoresen/RTM)* from Dover to Oostende and therejoin the "Nord Express" for the overnight run to Copenhagen. This train has the advantage of having first- and second-class sleeping cars as well as couchettes. Reservation is obligatory on this service.

The "Nord-West Express" during the summer has through carriages from the Hook of Holland to Stockholm and this makes things very simple. The train re-starts from Copenhagen at 8.15 A.M. (day 2 from London) and pulls into Stockholm at 4.45 P.M. (one hour later outside main summer season). During summer a 10.15 A.M. departure time gets you in at 6.45 P.M. The train carries a restaurant car from Helsingborg to Stockholm.

The "Holland-Scandinavia Express" doesn't have any through coaches for Stockholm, but there is a conveniently timed connecting service which leaves Copenhagen at 10.20 P.M. and runs overnight to the Swedish capital, arriving there at 7.30 the following morning (day 3 from London). The train has first- and second-class sleeping cars, and second-class couchettes, and day carriages. Alternatively, use the later departure from Copenhagen at 11.20 P.M.

Alternatively you can reach Stockholm by using the *DFDS* service from Harwich to Gothenburg and then continue by train and bus across Sweden. The ferry service runs on three or four days a week and the sea crossing takes about 24 hours. *British Rail* runs a connecting boat-train service to Harwich from London's Liverpool Street Station, and there is an hourly train service from Gothenburg to Stockholm. Buses to and from Stockhom connect at the Gothenburg quayside terminal with all *DFDS* Harwich sailings. The journey takes seven hours and stops are made at a number of important centers en route, including Borås and Norrköping. On this route schedules vary from sailing to sailing so check carefully with *DFDS*.

 FROM THE U.K. BY BUS. There are few bus services from the U.K., but a four-times-weekly *International Express* service is operated from London to Malmö, Gothenburg and Stockholm by Grey Green Coaches of London in conjunction with Bovo Tours of the Netherlands and GDG Continentbus of Sweden. During the winter the service runs twice weekly. It is routed across the Channel from Dover to Oostende, then through Belgium, the Netherlands and Germany to Travemünde on the Baltic, where you board the ferry to the Swedish port of Trelleborg. Journey time from London to Malmö is about 37 hours, 41 hours to Gothenburg and 47 hours to Stockholm. Bookings through International Express, The Coach Travel Center, 13 Regent St., London S.W.1 (tel. 01–439 9368). There is also a weekly summer service from London Victoria Coach Station to Stockholm. Details from Grey Green Coaches, 53 Stamford Hill, London N.16 (tel. 01–800 8010).

FROM THE U.K. BY CAR. This can be a delightful journey, especially if you enjoy sea trips, as many of the ships sailing to Scandinavian ports are really mini-liners. Alternatively, if you wish to keep the sea crossings to a minimum, use one of the shorter North Sea or English Channel crossings and then drive up through Holland and Germany to Denmark and then on to Sweden. However, remember that all this takes time, and you should carefully consider one of the numerous fly-drive packages, either with or without hotel accommodations.

There are two direct ferry services to Sweden from the U.K., both operated by *DFDS* and both running to Gothenburg. One, from Harwich, runs three or four times a week and takes 24 hours. The second is a twice weekly sailing from Newcastle and runs summer only; this takes slightly longer. In 1987, fares should work out at around £290 one way for a car, driver and one passenger (including cabin).

If you decide to drive up through Germany there are several ferry services to Sweden. A *Stena Line* ferry makes the crossing from Kiel to Gothenburg daily; contact Townsend Thoresen for details. *TT Line* have two services daily from Travemünde to Trelleborg on the southernmost tip of Sweden. On this route *Olau Line* offer a special low fare when combined with their service from Sheerness to Vlissingen. The crossing takes seven hours.

There is no problem reaching Sweden if you want to drive through Denmark first. A regular ferry shuttle operated by *Scandinavian Ferry Lines* runs from Dragør (just south of Copenhagen) to Limhamn, near Malmö, while farther north a service is operated every 15 minutes on the short crossing from Helsingør to Helsingborg by Scandinavian Ferry Lines in conjunction with Danish State Railways. There is also a service between Grenå in northern Jutland and Varberg on Sweden's west coast, operated by Lion Ferry, which also has a service from Grenå to Helsingborg. The most northerly crossing is from Frederikshavn to Gothenburg, run by Stena Line. Many of these services can be booked in advance through *DFDS*, 199 Regent Street, London W.1 (tel. 0255–552000).

CUSTOMS. Residents of non-European countries may bring duty-free into Sweden 400 cigarettes or 200 cigarillos or 100 cigars or 500 grams of tobacco; plus, 1 liter of spirits and 1 liter of wine *or* 2 liters of beer; plus a reasonable amount of perfume; plus, goods to the value of SEK 600.

Residents of European countries may bring duty-free into Sweden, if they are 15 or over, 200 cigarettes or 100 cigarillos or 50 cigars or 250 grams of tobacco; plus, for visitors aged 20 or more, 1 liter of spirits, 1 liter of wine and 2 liters of beer; plus, a reasonable amount of perfume; plus, goods to the value of SEK 600.

Alcoholic beverages over 60° (120°) may not be imported.

There is no limit to the amount of foreign currency that may be imported or exported, but no more than SEK 6,000 may be imported or exported.

Staying in Sweden

HOTELS. Hotel standards in Sweden are generally very high, even in the lowest price categories. As well as the larger and more expensive establishments—in almost every town you will find a "Grand Hotel," "Stadshotellet," or "Stora Hotellet"—the country is well provided with inexpensive guesthouses and pensions. In addition, all cities and most towns have a centrally-located hotel booking office *(Hotellcentral* or *Rumsförmedling)*, usually operated by the local tourist office. Nonetheless, advance reservations, particularly in larger towns, are recommended during the high season (May 15 to Sept. 30).

Prices can be high, but many hotels offer discounted rates all week during the summer and at weekends during the winter, while some chains offer special deals which can be booked through travel agencies in advance. The SARA group, for example, has a Scandinavian BonusPass, which costs $17 and entitles the holder to discounts ranging between 15% and 40% at some 100 first-class hotels, not only in Sweden but also in Denmark, Norway, Finland and Iceland. The pass is valid for an unlimited number of overnight stays from June 1 through August 31.

The Scandic Hotel group, which has hotels in 68 locations throughout Scandinavia, has a hotel check scheme which enables you to pay for your accommodation in advance. Weekend Checks are valid every weekend in all Scandic hotels from January through April and from mid-September to the year-end, while Summer Checks are valid every day between early May and mid-September. The 1987 price was about $23 per person per night, including breakfast, for Weekend Checks and $28 for Summer Checks, but supplements are payable at some city-center hotels.

Alternatively, a Biltur-Logi pass is good for even more inexpensive accommodations at 250 hotels in Sweden. The pass, available in both shops and all participating hotels, costs SEK 50 and qualifies you for bed-and-breakfast accommodations in any of the member hotels. Reservations can only be made one day in advance. Contact *Biltur-Logi,* Siljansgården, S-79 303 Tällberg for details.

Prices. We have divided all the hotels we list into four categories—Deluxe (L), Expensive (E), Moderate (M) and Inexpensive (I). These grades are determined solely by price.

Two people in a double room can expect to pay (prices in SEK)

Deluxe	950 and up
Expensive	750–950
Moderate	550–750
Inexpensive	300–550

These prices include breakfast and a 15% service charge. The abbreviations AE, DC, MC, and V stand for American Express, Diner's Club, Mastercard (including Acess and EuroCard), and Visa (Barclaycard).

CAMPING. Sweden boasts around 700 campsites, about 200 of which are open all year round. Most, however, are open from mid-May to late September. All camp sites are inspected and classified—from one to three stars—by the Swedish Tourist Board and all authorized sites display a green sign with a white "C" against a black tent. Most sites are located by the sea or a lake and facilities such as mini-golf, windsurfing, riding and tennis are common.

Charges range from SEK 40 to 60 per tent. An international camping carnet is required for all sites; alternatively, buy a Swedish Camping Card at any site. The Swedish Tourist Board publishes an abbreviated list of camping sites, in English.

For those who fancy the simple life but draw the line at being under canvas, some 250 sites also have "camping cottages" for hire. These have between two and four beds. Top prices are around SEK 250 per night. Sheets and blankets can be rented at camp sites; alternatively, bring your own.

YOUTH HOSTELS. There are around 300 youth hostels in Sweden, all operated by the Swedish Touring Club (STF). Hostels range from simple, student-type accommodations to restored manor houses and, in the case of the *af Chapman* in Stockholm, a restored sailing ship. Some can provide lunch and dinner, as well as breakfast, and a number also have hot and cold running water in every room. Linen may be rented in all hostels.

Members of organizations affiliated to the International Youth Hostels Federation are entitled to special low rates, but hostels in Sweden are otherwise open to all, regardless of age. It is generally advisable to make reservations in advance. Prices per night range from SEK 35 to 50. For further details, contact the Swedish Tourist Board or the *Swedish Touring Club,* PO Box 25, S-101 20 Stockholm (08790 32 00).

RESTAURANTS. Swedish restaurants, especially in more cosmopolitan centers, are varied both in style and price. At the top end of the spectrum, especially in Stockholm, you will find restaurants the equal of those anywhere in the world, while lower down the scale restaurants are generally of a high standard if somewhat more expensive than in the U.S.

Fast food of every variety is now available everywhere. Similarly, Chinese and Greek restaurants—all generally inexpensive—abound. Alternatively, anywhere calling itself a Bar will also provide self-service food but not, confusingly, alcohol.

Away from larger centers, the majority of restaurants are in hotels, though you will still find the occasional regular spot. Many restaurants also provide "office menus," or *dagens rätt;* (dish of the day); these normally cost SEK 35–40 and include a main dish, salad, beer or milk, bread and butter, coffee and service. Alcohol is generally very expensive in all restaurants.

The Swedish *smörgåsbord,* someone once said, is often abused in spelling, pronunciation and preparation. *Smörgåsbordet* is a large table usually placed in the middle of the dining room and easily accessible to all guests. It is piled high with a large number of delicacies to which you help yourself as often as you like. To appreciate it properly, however, the various dishes should be eaten in proper succession and not helter-skelter. Traditionally, the order goes something like this: pickled herring (possibly more than one kind) with a boiled potato; a couple more fish courses, probably cold smoked salmon, fried Baltic Sea herring, and sardines in oil; the meats, liver paste, boiled ham, sliced beef, not uncommonly smoked reindeer; a salad, fruit and/or vegetable; and finally the cheeses. Bread and butter is served throughout.

Prices. We have divided the restaurants in our listings into three categories: Expensive (E), Moderate (M) and Inexpensive (I). These grades are determined solely by price.

Prices, per person, excluding drinks (in SEK)

Expensive	160 and up
Moderate	80–160
Inexpensive	40–80

All prices are inclusive of service.

TIPPING. Tipping in hotels, restaurants and bars is not generally necessary in Sweden as the service charge is always included in your check. However, exceptional service may warrant a tip. Similarly, many round up restaurant bills to the nearest 5 or 10 kronor. There are only two exceptions to the no-tipping rule. Taxi drivers—who pay tax on tips whether they get them or not—should always be given between 10% and 15%. And give coat check attendants in restaurants around SEK 5. Otherwise, tipping is the exception rather than the rule.

MAIL. Post offices are open from 9 to 6 Monday to Friday and 9 to 1 on Saturdays. During the summer, some do not open on Saturdays. Aside from post offices, you can also buy stamps from the machines outside post offices, in department stores and hotels. These take 1 and 5 krona coins. Similarly, some shops selling postcards also sell stamps. Mail boxes are painted a distinctive yellow.

Postal rates for airmail letters under 20 grams to the U.S. are SEK 3.40, and SEK 2.90 to Europe; postcards to the U.S. are SEK 2.90, and to Europe SEK 2.30.

CLOSING TIMES. Shops are generally open 9–6, Mon. to Fri. On Sat. and the day before a holiday, closing time varies between 1 and 4. Department stores and many other shops in the larger cities stay open until 8 or 10 one evening in the week (usually Mon. or Fri.), but not in June or July. Some of the larger stores open on Sun. Banks are open 9.30–3.00 Mon. to Fri.; many also open in the evening, 4.30–6.00. In many larger cities, banks are open 9.30–5.30. The bank at Stockholm's Arlanda International Airport is open daily from 7 A.M. to 10 P.M.

TAX-FREE SHOPPING. About 10,000 Swedish shops —500 in Stockholm alone—participate in a tax-free shopping scheme for visitors enabling you to save around 15% on all buys exported within one week of purchase. Take your passport with you to shops and ask for the special tax-free receipt. All airports and ports have repayment offices which will refund in cash—deducting a 5% service charge—the tax paid. In some cases the refunds are made on board the ferries. Complementing this scheme is the Sweden Card, which costs SEK 150 and gives a further 5% cash refund on all tax-free purchases, as well as discounts on services like car rental.

For further details, contact the Swedish Tourist Board, or call (0410) 19560 once in Sweden.

Getting Around Sweden

BY AIR. Sweden has a good internal air network, with *SAS* and *LIN* (Linjeflyg) the main carriers. To give a rough idea of flying times, Stockholm to Kiruna, north of the Arctic Circle, takes around 90 minutes, while Stockholm to Gothenburg, on the west coast, takes around 55 minutes.

Outside peak times, there are many fare bargains to be had. All off-peak fares are some 30% below peak rates for one-way trips. Similarly, senior citizens pay only SEK 200 on all one-way fares in offpeak periods.

Anyone planning to stay away for more than two nights or over a Saturday or Sunday night is entitled to a "mini-fare," valid only for round trips using specified flights. This gives a 50% discount, and in addition your wife or husband and young people between 15 and 25 traveling with you pay only SEK 200 each (plus an extra SEK 100 if a change of flights in Stockholm is necessary), while the fare for children between 2 and 11 is SEK 100. The demand for "mini-fare" tickets is very great, especially in the summer, so be sure to book well in advance. Those under 26 are also entitled to special standby fares of only SEK 150 on all one-way trips (SEK 250 on some longer routes).

Finally, both airlines operate good-value fly-drive schemes over the summer and at weekends throughout the year. But you must book your car at the same time as you reserve your seat.

BY TRAIN. Swedish trains are comfortable, clean and reliable with efficient express services linking all main cities. First and second class carriages and dining or self-service cars are carried on most trains. Sleeping cars

—costing from about SEK 100 in addition to the normal fare—and couchettes —costing approximately SEK 70—are also available on all overnight runs. No smoking rules must be strictly observed. Note also that the letter "R" in timetables means that seat reservations—SEK 15—are required.

Rail fares in Sweden are suprisingly inexpensive. There is now a price ceiling for long-distance trips, with a flat-rate fare for all journeys of about 560 miles and over. Children under 16 travel at half the applicable fare. There is also a special fare for groups of between two and five passengers. The first adult pays the normal fare but additional adults qualify for a substantial discount and the first child travels free. Passengers holding the European senior citizens' railcard qualify for a 50% reduction on Swedish rail fares.

Swedish Railways has a special first-class 'go-as-you-please" card which at presstime (mid-1987) cost SEK 750 for one week's unlimited travel anywhere on the system between mid-June and mid-Aug., or SEK 1,250 for two weeks (children half-price).

In addition to these exclusively Swedish discounts, the *Nordturist* (or Scandrail card), the *Inter-Rail* card, the *Eurailpass* and *Eurail Youthpass,* and the *Rail Europ Senior Card* are all valid within Sweden. See "Getting Around Scandinavia by Rail" in *Planning Your Trip* for further details.

BY CAR. Given its vast size and the excellence of the air and rail network, car travel in Sweden may seem a less than ideal means of getting around, especially as only main roads, particularly in the north of the country, are paved, all others being gravel. Having said this, however, roads are very well engineered, and the small population also means that there is generally very little traffic. Similarly, there are no toll roads anywhere.

There are strict speed limits, however, even outside built-up areas. These are 110, 90 or 70 km.p.h. (68, 56 or 43 m.p.h.). In built-up areas the speed limit is always 50 km.p.h. (31 m.p.h.), and 30 km.p.h. (19 m.p.h.) outside schools. Speed limits are always well sign-posted. Towing a trailer with brakes, the limit is 70 km.p.h. (43 m.p.h.); without brakes, it is 40 km.p.h. (25 m.p.h.).

Note also that seat belts are compulsory for drivers and front seat passengers and that you must *always* use dipped headlights, both at night and during the day. U.S. drivers' licenses are valid in Sweden.

Parking restrictions are strictly observed. You should always park only in designated areas. Parking meters accept one krona coins. Wrongly-parked cars will be towed away.

The best people to try in the event of a breakdown are the police or "Larmtjänst," a 24-hour service run by the Swedish insurance companies, with branches all over the country. Alternatively, for emergencies call 90 000; for less drastic help, call 08–241000 or 0760–40065. English is always spoken.

Finally, it is very important to observe the extremely strict (and equally strictly-enforced) drink/drive regulations. Anything in excess of two bottles of beer will be enough for a conviction, and tests are made frequently. Fines are very heavy and imprisonment by no means rare. On the whole, the smart thing is simply not to drink if you're driving.

BY BUS. Swedish buses are run by the national rail network and a small number of private companies. Prices are very low, but services relatively slow. In more remote parts of the country, however, a reasonable Post Bus service knits the scattered communities together.

BY BICYCLE. Bikes can be rented throughout Sweden. For a complete list of rental companies, write *Cykelfrämjandet,* P.O. Box 30 70, S-103 61, Stockholm, which also publishes a useful guide in English to cycling vacations in Sweden. The *Swedish Touring Club*, P.O. Box 25, S-101, 20 Stockholm, can also provide details of organized bike tours in practically every province. Prices are very reasonable.

Many buses and trains will also carry bikes free of charge; inquire at tourist offices or write *Svenska Cykelsällskapet*, P.O. Box 6006, S-163 06, Spånga, for details.

Leaving Sweden

 CUSTOMS ON RETURNING HOME. If you propose to take on your holiday any *foreign-made* articles, such as cameras, binoculars, expensive timepieces and the like, it is wise to put with your travel documents the receipt from the retailer or some other evidence that the item was bought in your home country. If you bought the article on a previous holiday abroad and have already paid duty on it, carry with you the receipt for this. Otherwise, on returning home, you may be charged duty (for British residents, Value Added Tax as well). In other words, unless you can prove prior possession, foreign-made articles are dutiable *each time* they enter the U.S. The details below are correct as we go to press. It would be wise to check in case of change.

American residents who are out of the U.S.A. at least 48 hours and have claimed no exemption during the previous 30 days are entitled to bring in duty-free up to $400 worth of bona fide gifts or items for their own personal use. Do not think that *already used* will exempt an item. If you buy clothing abroad and wear it during your travels it will nonetheless be dutiable when you reenter the U.S.

The $400 duty free allowance is based on the full fair *retail* value of the goods (previously, the customs' estimation was on the wholesale value). You must now list the items purchased and *they must accompany you when you return*. So keep all receipts handy with the detailed list, and pack the goods together in one case. The $50 mailed gift-scheme (see below) is also based on the retail value. Every member of a family is entitled to this same exemption, regardless of age, and their exemptions can be pooled. Infants and children get the same exemptions as adults, except for alcoholic beverages and tobacco. Beyond the first $400 worth of goods, inspectors now assess a flat 10% duty on the next $1,000 worth; above $1,400 duties vary according to the kind of merchandise.

One quart of alcoholic beverages and up to 100 cigars (non-Cuban!) may be included in the exemption if you are 21 years of age or older. There is no limitation on the number of cigarettes you bring in for your personal use, regardless of age. Alcoholic beverages in excess of one quart are subject to customs duty and internal revenue tax. Approximate rates are (1/5 gallon); brandy or liquor, $2–$3; champagne, 90¢; wine, 15¢. The importation must not be in violation of the laws of the state of arrival. Furthermore, your tobacco and alcohol may be reported to the authorities in your own home state, to be taxed by them.

Only one bottle of certain perfumes that are trademarked in the United States (Lanvin, Chanel, etc.) may be brought in unless you can completely obliterate the trademark on the bottle, or get written permission from the manufacturer to bring more. Other perfumes are limited by weight or value. The specialized Paris houses will give you the complete list.

Foreign visitors to the U.S. (nonresidents), and U.S. military personnel returning from duty abroad should inquire separately about regulations and exemptions pertaining to them.

American rates of customs duty may change, so it is best to check the regulations with the nearest American Embassy during your visit. There are special Customs advisors at the U.S. embassies in London, Paris, Rome and Bonn and at the Consulate in Frankfurt. In general, of course, narcotics, pornography, seditious materials, and dangerous articles (fireworks, poisons, switchblades) are forbidden in the U.S.

You do not have to pay duty on art objects or antiques, provided they are over 100 years old. Remember this and ask the dealer who sells you that Sheffield plate or that 17th-century Dutch landscape for a certificate establishing its age. But when you buy, remember also that some countries regulate the removal of cultural properties and works of art.

Gifts which cost less than $50 may be mailed to friends or relatives at home, but not more than one per day (of receipt) to any one addressee. Mark the package: Unsolicited Gift—value less than $50. These gifts must not include perfumes costing more than $1, tobacco or liquor; however, they do not count as part of your $400 exemption.

Do not bring home foreign meats, fruits, plants, soil, or other agricultural items when you return to the United States. To do so will delay you at the port of entry. It is illegal to bring in foreign agricultural items without permission, because they can spread destructive plant or animal pests and diseases. For more information, read the pamphlet "Customs Hints," or write to: "Quarantines," Department of Agriculture, Federal Center Bldg., Hyattsville, MD 20782, and ask for Program Aid No. 1083, entitled "Traveler's Tips on Bringing Food, Plant and Animal Products into the United States."

Procedures for customs and immigration have been greatly simplified recently. Customs declaration forms are distributed on your plane or ship before you arrive. If your purchases are worth no more than $400 you fill out only the identification portions of the form and make an oral declaration when you pass the inspector. If you have over $400 worth you must make a written declaration. Under the Citizens Bypass Program, American citizens can show their passports to the customs inspector and eliminate the separate inspection by an immigration officer.

Canadian residents may, in addition to personal effects, bring in the following duty free: a maximum of 50 cigars, 200 cigarettes, 2 pounds of tobacco and 40 ounces of liquor, provided these are declared in writing to customs on arrival and accompany the traveler in hand or checked-through baggage. These are included in the basic exemption of $300 a year or $100 per quarter. Personal gifts should be mailed as "Unsolicited Gift—Value Under $40." Canadian customs regulations are strictly enforced; you should check what your allowances are and to make sure you have kept receipts for whatever you have bought abroad. For details ask for the Canada Customs brochure, *I Declare*.

British residents face two levels of duty free allowance entering the U.K.; one, for goods bought outside the EEC or for goods bought in a duty free shop within the EEC; two, for goods bought in an EEC country but not in a duty free shop.

In the first category you may import duty free: 200 cigarettes or 100 cigarillos or 50 cigars or 250 grammes of tobacco (*Note* if you live outside Europe, these allowances are doubled); plus one liter of alcoholic drinks over 22% vol. (38.8% proof) or two liters of alcoholic drinks not over 22% vol. or fortified or sparkling wine; plus two liters of still table wine; plus 50 grammes of perfume; plus nine fluid ounces of toilet water; plus other goods to the value of £32.

In the second category you may import duty free: 300 cigarettes or 150 cigarillos or 75 cigars or 400 grammes of tobacco; plus 1½ liters of alcoholic drinks over 22% vol. (38.8% proof) or three liters of alcoholic drinks not over 22% vol. or fortified or sparkling wine; plus five liters of still table wine; plus 75 grammes of perfume; plus 13 fluid ounces of toilet water; plus other goods to the value of £250. (*Note* though it is not classified as an alcoholic drink by EEC countries for Customs' purposes and is thus considered part of the "other goods" allowance, you may not import more than 50 liters of beer).

In addition, no animals or pets of any kind may be brought into the U.K. The penalties for doing so are severe and are strictly enforced; there are *no* exceptions. Similarly, fresh meats, plants and vegetables, controlled drugs and firearms and ammunition may not be brought into the U.K. There are no restrictions on the import or export of British and foreign currencies.

Anyone planning to stay in the U.K. for more than six months should contact H.M. Customs and Excise, Kent House, Upper Ground, London S.E.1 (tel. 01–928 0533) for further information.

PRELUDE TO SWEDEN

Dolls' Houses in the Wilderness

by
ANDREW BROWN

Because Sweden is the largest and the richest of the Scandinavian countries, it is also the most typical: any idea of what is "Scandinavian" is informed by Sweden. If the other countries differ from the Swedish model, this tends to suggest that they are not truly "Scandinavian."

The word suggests a combination of gloom and cleanliness; efficiency combined with joyless affluence, conjuring up a vision of somewhere very impressive, but not really suited to human life. Elks and mosquitoes thrive; other lifeforms do not.

It is easy enough to find parts of Sweden that correspond to this stereotype—and they are almost certainly the first parts that the tourist will see. But the tension and the interest of Swedish life comes from the fact that the Swedes themselves could no more stand to live as they seem to do than anybody else could. If the foreigner recoils from certain aspects of Swedish life, so do the Swedes themselves. The result can be extremely confusing, but it is both more interesting and a great deal more pleasant than the rather inhuman front presented to the world would suggest. The moral, for anyone who wants to enjoy Sweden—and there is much here to enjoy—is 'Get off the Main Street'.

The Minor Arts of Peace

A perfect example of this is provided by Uddevalla, a town on the west coast that looks from the main road like every other town in Sweden. Admittedly, there is nowhere in Europe but Stockholm where you will find towns that look good from a four-lane highway, but the drabness of Uddevalla is remarked upon even by guidebooks.

Between the main road and the sea is a low-lying area that floods after westerly gales every year. Every fall the octagonal tourist office in Uddevalla is surrounded by water and accessible only to those tourists who had the foresight to pack canoes or waders. It makes an annual splash on the TV news.

On the other side of the road, the town itself is concealed by a line of modern developments: car lots and demolition sites, and large grey concrete buildings that look like overgrown Lego models without either the color or the imagination of the originals.

Seeing all this, the average traveler gets away down the highway as quickly as possible. He may admire the engineering that has made the highway possible, but if he thinks anything at all about the town, it is only that Uddevalla is one of those places that Nature meant to be bypassed. But the wise man turns off the main road into the town, and gets lost in the one-way system. The belt of nastiness is only one block deep. The buildings behind are not particularly beautiful, but they are not inhuman. One conceals a rocky garden, where you can sit on terraces drinking beer all through the summer twilight, moving occasionally to keep within the shade of trees. The streets are crowded with people, not with cars. There is an openair market. A little more exploration discovers a comfortable cafe, and a shop that sells foreign newspapers. An indoor market sells fish so fresh their eyes and flanks still gleam. Much more surprisingly, it sells kippers, which you can only otherwise buy in Great Britain. These are the minor arts of peace. They may not be spectacular, but they're important; and very well done throughout Scandinavia, but to find them in Sweden you must go behind the facade of grey modernity.

In a Meadow by a Lake

The town of Uddevalla, however, is still public Sweden. Even after you have learned to find and enjoy the shops and cafes, the houses on the hills around remain closed and mysterious. The less privacy people have, the more closely they guard it. To discover what makes Swedes tick, you must go still further from the main road, perhaps to a house that stands some miles south of Uddevalla. It's not a tourist attraction: in fact it is a private house, though people are encouraged to visit the lakes and the woods around it. And those with a taste for the outdoor life can spend a night in the cabin across the meadow.

The house is not far from the main road, but you must travel for some time to get there. The branch road starts at a modern gas station on a highway, leads past a couple of supermarkets and then a much older general store. When it climbs into the hills there is no metalled surface. In the space of a mile you have traveled back 30 years. Five miles of gravel road lead to a track through the forest that only a tractor could get down.

The woods around are typical of Southern Sweden. They seem un-tamed—elk hairs lie in clumps along the tracks—but they are not oppressive. The lack of undergrowth makes the forest seem extraor-dinarily spacious, and though the trees are almost all conifers, they're not monotonous. No one who has not seen a Scandinavian forest in early summer can imagine how many shades of green there are in the world, each one distinct and bright and clear. The elements of the view are limited, but they are never quite the same; which keeps the forest beautiful however far you walk, but makes it very easy to get lost in. So be a little careful.

The house stands at the end of this track, in a meadow by a lake. It was built 50 years ago by two Finnish lumberjacks, who lived what must have been a life of monotony remarkable even by the standards of immigrant Finnish lumberjacks. In winter they worked in the for-ests; in summer they netted pike out of the lake and sold what they could not eat. Eventually they moved away. The house fell into dis-repair. This is an old pattern. You *can* live off the land in Sweden, but few would choose to do so. (In the 19th century, Sweden was so poor that a quarter of all the descendants of Swedes living then are now Americans). Walking through the woods in the south of the country you will often come across the remains of cabins from this time, their stone foundations worn down like old teeth.

Even the lake where the lumberjacks had netted their pike died, poisoned by acid rain. The prevailing winds from England and Germa-ny are loaded with sulphur dioxide from factories and car exhausts. This turns to weak sulphuric acid and falls on Sweden, where the peat and granite cannot buffer it as English soil can. The snow that looks so pure in winter is actually weak sulphuric acid, frozen, fluffy, and deadly. When it melts each spring, four months' worth of acid runs into the lakes and rivers in a week, killing fish fry and eggs, most forms of algae, and most insects too. The lakes are neatly sterilized. Of the thousand or so lakes in Bohuslän, only a handful can now support any lifeform higher than the water-louse.

So far this story has dealt with the effects of the country on the people who live there. The point, however, is how they have changed the country. In the early 70s the house and the lake were taken over by a group of local fishermen. They filled the lakes with trout—each one of which had to be carried down the track in rucksacks full of water—and arranged to have lime spread on the ice each spring to counteract the acid rain. All this is paid for by selling fishing permits for the lakes, but by this time catching fish had become a secondary consideration for the fishermen. Their treasure was the house.

It has been lovingly restored, with stripped and polished pine floors, prints and ornamental driftwood on the walls. It seems that the attrac-tion is that they can get away from all respectable life here. They can drink all night and not worry about driving in the morning; they can chop wood and cover themselves with paint; they chew tobacco and spit into an open fire. It is a small boys' paradise, and irresistible to anyone over the age of 15.

But these small boys in their 30s and 40s turn into old maids in the morning. They tiptoe around in their socks, brushing and sweeping; they agonize over the exact placement of a hat-stand; they would, if they could, reintroduce the death penalty for littering. The wilderness camp is turned into a dolls' house.

It is this clearing up that is the point of the whole thing. This is Sweden in microcosm. The fishermen do not go into the woods to get away from it all, but to extend it all: to build a perfect, private society together in the middle of nowhere. All Swedish life is best understood as conducted in dolls' houses in the wilderness, and it demands of its participants the same passion and concentration as a children's game.

Just as heroism is the Polish vice, sincerity is the curse of the Swedes. They can believe anything—and they do—but this belief is almost always a communal activity. Swedes in discussion are like a shoal of fish. They all point in the same direction, and if they change direction, all do so at once. Sometimes they split into competing shoals, but within each group the discipline remains. What's rare in Sweden, and always seems slightly ridiculous, are self-sufficient individuals, or, if you like, lone fish.

How to Move a Mountain

These attitudes are easily misunderstood. Because belief—sincerity —comes so naturally to the Swedes, they may seem to outsiders insincere, just as the girl who can't say "No" seems incapable of loving because she falls in love so easily. But this is unfair. If the sceptical British, for example, strike ridiculous attitudes, they are being hypocritical. If the Swedish do the same, this is not hypocrisy, but wholly sincere self-deception. And they could easily justify this quirk of character if they ever felt the need to justify something that is to them so self-evident. Faith *has* moved mountains in Sweden, most obviously in the iron-mining town of Kiruna, above the Arctic Circle.

But there is no need to go as far as Kiruna to see this, even though it is one of the most remarkable towns in the world. Stockholm itself is best enjoyed as the most beautiful dolls' house in the world. The most famous sights of the city all have this quality of toys: there is the restored 17th-century warship, the *Wasa;* the royal palace, for show rather than for living in; the openair museum at Skansen, where houses, churches, and workshops from all over Sweden have been re-erected on the slopes around a zoo. In the workshops there are real craftsmen playing at being real craftsmen; in the zoo there are wolverines and seals playing in beautifully landscaped enclosures.

The modern center of the city is extremely ugly, but this, too, is the result of a communal fantasy. This was the dream of the American '50s (and the Swedish '60s) that with enough money and enough cars, everyone would be happy if there were no buildings in sight more than five years old to remind them of what they had lost. The tourist office in Sweden House marks the furthest outpost of this dream. Beyond it lies a park—the Kungsträdgården—and when the city council proposed to ruin that, too, for the sake of a new subway station, mass demonstrations stopped the plan. Respectable Swedes, who would tell you even then that they were the most buttoned-up and formal people in the world, climbed the trees that were to be cut down, and clung to the branches with the workmen poised below, axes at the ready, until the city council gave way, as they were forced to do. Opposition broke the spell; when communal belief was no longer possible, the ideas that had laid waste the city center lost all their power.

This is not to say that all modern Swedish architecture is ugly; odd bits of it are extremely beautiful, though nowhere as lovely as in Finland. But again, this beauty is to be found in hidden places, not in public ones. The beautiful public buildings of Stockholm are all old, and almost all of them are built at the edge of islands which greatly increase their beauty.

Angst and Elks

Of course, one of the things the visitor to Stockholm expects to see is porn. This is most odd for anyone who lives in Sweden—we cannot imagine how the legend of "Swedish Sin" arose. There was admittedly a period in the late '60s when the Swedes decided that since pornography is unavoidable, it must be good for you. That decision later came to seem foolish. Now they are just confused, but not very worried. The guilt, fear, and anguish that Anglo-Saxons lavish on sex are devoted by the Swedes to alcohol.

The Swedish attitude to drink is one of the things that most intensely irritates the foreigner. Drink is not so much difficult as inconvenient to obtain; in those few restaurants that serve it, it is extremely expensive. An elaborate network of law and tabu has almost eliminated drunken driving, except for those drivers too drunk to remember the consequences. This may have kept death off the roads (elks cause more car crashes every year in Sweden than ever humans do) but it has also eliminated social drinking, except in large towns. No amount of pleasure is worth the risk of losing your license in a country where cars are as common and as vital as they are in Sweden. In the countryside there is no-one who can afford to drink with strangers except the town drunk, and who would want to drink with him?

It sometimes seems that the Swedes cannot enjoy a drink unless they are convinced that it is harming them. The windows of the state liquor stores are lined with anti-alcohol posters displayed behind ramparts of a purplish fluid called *Schloss Boosenburg,* an "alcohol-free wine." But things are loosening up nowadays, largely as a result of the introduction of real wine, which women can drink and enjoy with men. The old Swedish tabus on drink had a partially sexual underpinning: men drank; women picked up the pieces, and resented having to do so. This was clearly unsatisfactory, though it did produce one marvellous recipe: Put a small silver coin in the bottom of a cup; add sweetened black coffee till you can no longer see the coin; then pour in vodka until the coin becomes visible again. This is not a drink for those who wish to remain gentlemen in their cups.

It's worth dwelling on this subject because the tabus of a country are more informative even than the local newspapers. The superstitious horror with which the Swedes regarded drink is really a result of the facts that drunks quarrel. They forget the rules of the communal game, and stumble through the dolls' house, breaking things and shouting, interrupting everybody else. No wonder their fellows turn on them with the ferocity of children. For a children's game has power only when all the players believe in it. Otherwise the dolls have no life, and will quickly be broken.

This need not worry the visitor. The Swedes treat foreigners with great courtesy and kindness. Almost all of them speak English, and all are delighted to show you their splendid game. They will perhaps complain that theirs is the most regulated and tightly controlled society in the Western world; and in a sense they are right. For the last 12 years, the Swedish parliament has been passing laws and regulations at a rate of one every eight hours of the day and night, or more than 1,000 a year. But for the most part the citizens treat this activity as lightly as do the parliamentarians themselves. The system has reached such a pitch of complication that no-one takes very much notice of it any more. The Swedes obey such rules as they feel are sensible, and ignore the others. They feel entitled to do so because it is, after all, their game. This sense of belonging makes them a very restful people to be among; nor can anyone who has known a Swedish summer feel that there is anywhere in the world that is more beautiful in the months of May and June.

Detail from Picture-stone, Gotland, 8th century.

SWEDISH HISTORY

Prosperity Out of Conflict

In the beginning were the glaciers that lay over the whole Scandinavian peninsula and that crushed it down beneath frozen sea. Parts of this land were still rising in historically recent times: the surface of Lake Mälaren fell four meters during the Middle Ages, and the fertile valleys to the north of the lake (on whose outlet Stockholm stands) did not completely emerge until the later Iron Age in around A.D. 500. In this region, the province of Uppland, the Swedes first began to distinguish themselves from other Scandinavian tribes.

The Terrain of the Swedes

The first inhabitants of Scandinavia, living along the fringes of the glaciers, as the Eskimos still do in northern Canada, seem to have reached the peninsula in about 6000 B.C., but we know nothing about them except that they did not farm, but hunted, fished, and gathered berries. It was not until the forests came to Scandinavia, and at about the same time, agriculture, that the culture from which the Swedes, the Danes, and the Norwegians were to differentiate themselves became clear.

It was the forests that determined the nature of the Swedes. The primeval forest that covered most of central and northern Sweden (fragments can still be admired in nature reserves) is practically impassable, and difficult to clear. Human settlements formed beside rivers and lakes. The valleys and the flat, alluvial plains could be worked with Iron Age ploughs. The water itself made communications possible and provided food. This ecology determined the social organization of Scandinavia which was made up of tribes, each with a leader, or kinglet, rather than nations, each with a king.

Though the present-day division of Scandinavia seems natural and logical, with each country divided from the others by sea or mountains, it is in fact a recent development. It was not until 1658 that treeless Blekinge, the southernmost province of Sweden, was captured from the Danes; and not until 1809 that Finland, until then a part of Sweden, was conquered by Russia. Though we think of water as dividing countries, and forests as insignificant obstacles, these roles were, however, reversed for most of Scandinavian history: water united and forests divided.

So the territory of the Danes formed round the sounds of the Kattegat, and the territory of the Swedes around Lake Mälaren. By about A.D. 100 we can distinguish these two tribes—and many others—in the works of the Roman historian Tacitus. The Suiones, or Svear as they called themselves, whose law and dialect were to become the kernel round which all modern Sweden grew, were tall men, Tacitus tells us, with great horses, and wonderful shining furs, which they traded. He does not tell us anything else, but then Scandinavia, for a Roman, was one of the heartlands of barbarism. No Roman army ever conquered or invaded it, and though the Romans exercised a great influence on Scandinavia (the common term for a small coin, öre, in all the Scandinavian languages derives from the Roman word for silver, *aureus*) this influence was always indirect.

Pagans and Vikings

Our knowledge of pagan, Germanic Scandinavia, is always derived from the outside and has a strong Christian bias. But we still know a certain amount about the people who were to become the Swedes. They spoke a Germanic language, Old Norse, which was common to most of Scandinavia.

The archeological record is rich. We know that the people who were to become the Swedes were fairly rich—at least their princes lived well, and were sometimes buried in great splendor. We know that they developed the Viking longship, a vessel which enabled them to strike and ravish the coastlines of northern Europe. We know something of the gods they worshipped, though most of our information comes from Icelandic sagas written 300 or 400 years later, and by that time Swedish history was quite distinct from that of the western Vikings. The God Ull, for example, hardly appears in the Icelandic tradition: yet he was worshipped widely in Sweden where his memory is still preserved in local names. The great athletics stadium in Gothenburg, for example, is at "Ullevi," meaning Ull's sacred place.

We know little about their Bronze Age predecessors, who have left only their mysterious pictures, scratched on rocks, of suns, boats, and ithyphallic heroes. (These are best seen at Tanumshede, north of Gothenburg.) So a chronological account of Swedish history had best start at around A.D. 700 in the Mälar valley, just before the dawn of the Viking Age.

The Mälar valley was prosperous and fertile at the beginning of this period. In Uppsala there was the great heathen temple, of which a

Christian chronicler says that it was covered with gold (which need not be believed) and that it was the scene of constant sacrifices (which there is no reason to doubt). A later missionary saw the whole sacred grove festooned with the hanged, rotting corpses of men and horses as well as smaller animals. At Birka, on an island in Lake Mälaren, a trading center was already established, with a fortress to guard it above. Furs and iron came from the interior; silver, slaves and cloth from over the seas. There were 2,000 farms in the region at the time and by the end of the Viking Age this number had doubled. Each farm is now reckoned to have supported about ten people.

Looting and Pillage

It was not hunger, or overpopulation, that drove the Vikings out, but an instinct for profitable adventure. In A.D. 800 the rest of Europe was exhausted and divided and the only coherent authority was provided by the Catholic Church. The Empire of Charlemagne, who was crowned the first Holy Roman Emperor by the Pope in 800, seemed to represent the triumph of the Church, and of those fragments of civilization which had survived the fall of Rome and the rise of Christianity. But it was a promise for the future and not a lasting triumph. When Charlemagne died his empire was divided among his children, and discord broke out immediately.

Power on the mainland of Europe at this time came from the stirrup, which allowed a mounted man to fight at close quarters in the saddle. Before stirrups came to Europe with the Goths (themselves originally from southern Sweden), cavalry was an unimportant adjunct to masses of disciplined infantry.

The Vikings did not fight on horseback. They rode ponies to the battlefield, and there they dismounted. But they had the enormous advantage of mobility. Their ships allowed them to deliver a force of armed men anywhere near water, more quickly than a defending army could move on land; and once disembarked, the Vikings were formidable fighters. They were usually well-fed, a rarity for armies of that age, and were brave, cunning, and completely ruthless. They were also well-armed. An Arab traveler, who came across a camp of Swedish Vikings in Russia, described how each man carried a sword, a dagger and an axe at all times—a habit he ascribed to their fear of each other's treachery.

At the beginning of the Viking Age, the Scandinavian tribes, or clans, could hardly be distinguished from each other. They all spoke the same language (Old Norse), and shared the same culture of slaughter and feasting. The names of some early Swedish Kings, though not many, have been preserved. There was King Sveigder, who offended a dwarf, who in turn led him by magic inside a boulder, where he was entombed; King Fjoiner, twice enviable, who drowned himself in a tub of mead and was subsequently deified.

The Vikings abroad tended to seek the sort of countryside that they came from. The Norwegians became the Vikings of the sea, and of the northern, rocky islands: the Faroes, Iceland, Greenland, and ultimately Newfoundland. The Danes plundered the fertile coastal strips of England and northern France. The Swedes were the Vikings of the forests, and the great forests lay to the east. The balance between trade and plunder in Viking life varied according to circumstance. The one inflexible principle was to take from the weak and sell to the strong.

The Swedes started their expansion at the mouths of the great rivers of the eastern Baltic. A group of fortified trading posts was built to command all the trade routes from modern Leningrad to Lithuania. Short portages bring one from these regions to the headwaters of the great rivers of southern Russia: the Dnieper, the Volga, and the Don. A Byzantine record has fortuitiously preserved the Norse names that these Vikings, known as Rus, or Varangians, gave to the seven great rapids of the lower Dnieper. But there is evidence to show that the Swedes had penetrated to Byzantium as early as 839, when a group of "Rhos" turned up at the Frankish court in what is now West Germany, in the company of a Byzantine emissary. The Frankish King discovered they were Swedes, who had traveled the whole way through Russia, across the Black Sea to Constantinople, and from there to France, since they feared the dangers of a return through Russia.

By the early 900s, no Swede need have feared the journey through Russia. A dynasty of Rus had established itself at Kiev, on the Dnieper, and it is to this dynasty that we owe the name "Russia." This may have been the greatest triumph of the Swedish Vikings. As is the way of triumphs, it also marked the beginning of the end. Within three generations, the "Rus" state had become Russian, a process made visible by the way in which princes' names took on Slav, rather than Norse, forms: Ingvar became Igor, Helge became Oleg, and so on.

> They traveled bravely
> Far after gold
> And Eastwards
> Fed the eagles.
> Died Southwards
> In Serkland

To feed the eagles means to kill enemies in battle. This runic epitaph from Gripsholm in Södermanland, commemorates one Harald, the son of Tola, who had the stone raised. Harald died on the last great Viking expedition eastwards, which is usually dated at 1041. His epitaph may stand for the whole Viking Age, which ended when the old style of warfare could no longer guarantee victory.

Another reason is suggested by the runestones raised over some of Harald's comrades. Many of these ask God and God's Mother to care for the dead. Sweden was becoming a Christian country. The first King to be baptized was Olof Skötkonung (The Protector) in 1008, but it was not until nearly 1200 that the whole country was Christianized, by a Norwegian King who led something between a plundering expedition and a crusade into Småland.

The Savagery of The Dark Ages

The transition from the Viking Age to the Middle Ages is shrouded in darkness. Where it is illuminated by the chroniclers, the medieval scene is one of terrible savagery. But even if the medieval, Christian Swedes were not noticeably better behaved than their pagan, Viking predecessors, they were better organized. Sweden had become a Kingdom—the Kingdom of the Svear and the Götar, the inhabitants of the forests of the south. The plains of Skåne and Blekinge remained Danish throughout the Middle Ages, and Bohuslän, the province to the west of the Göta River, remained Norwegian. But the forests of Finland were swiftly and bloodily conquered and Christianized by the Swedes. The Viking Kings had enriched themselves by plundering. The Medieval Kings taxed their own subjects instead. Taxation brought, in theory, laws and peace. Medieval Sweden was a stratified, though not exactly feudal, society, and its history can be read two ways: either as the history of the aristocracy, who were exempt from taxes, or as the history of the relations between the tax-gathering and eating classes, and the tax-paying peasant. These last constituted the majority of the population. They certainly constituted the majority of the free population. The story is unedifying however it is told. One example illustrates the table manners of the aristocracy. In 1317, King Magnus Eriksson of the Kolkunga dynasty, who had been forced to divide his kingdom with his two brothers, invited them to a winter feast at Nyköping Castle. When they had eaten and drunk their fill, and retired to bed, they were woken by the King's soldiers and taken to a dungeon where they were put in weighty fetters. Their followers revolted and when the King found he was losing the subsequent civil war, he had his imprisoned brothers starved to death. The last one to die was later found to have gnawed upon the shoulder of his brother's corpse.

The miseries of the peasantry were not perhaps so grotesque, but they were real enough. Between 1349 and 1352, for instance, the Black Death killed a third of the population of Norway, and about a quarter of the Swedish people. Nevertheless, the Middle Ages saw an increase in the number of settlements and farms and the development of the peasant village as the basic social unit which replaced the Viking clan. And it was during the Middle Ages, too, that the first national code of laws was promulgated, and the idea of a parliament began to emerge. This was an assembly of the magnates and larger peasants whose job it was to elect the King, and if possible to restrict his powers.

It was during this period that the copper and iron mining industries of Bergslagen were founded, but really, for the Swedes, the Middle Ages were a period of relative decline. The north no longer enjoyed the military and economic advantages it had had during the Viking Age, and power moved towards the southern fringes of Scandinavia, to Denmark, and the north German merchant cities of the Hansa League.

Reforming with the Reformation

In 1389, all the Scandinavian Kingdoms were united by the Treaty of Kalmar under Queen Margareta of Denmark. But this federation proved neither popular nor successful during the following century. Engelbrekt, an ironmaster probably from Dalecarlia, led a popular rebellion against foreigners and tax collectors in 1434; two years later he was treacherously murdered on a promontory in Lake Hjälmaren by a Swedish noble. This did not prevent him from becoming a national hero, and his rebellion a symbol of Swedish patriotism.

Confusion about the meaning of nationality was everywhere during the Middle Ages. Even Joan of Arc, who was to become the embodiment of France, was herself handed over to the English by Frenchmen who thought themselves patriotic. It was not until the Reformation and the end of the Middle Ages that nation states, as we now understand them, began to emerge.

The man who brought about this transition on Sweden was Gustav Vasa, a charismatic and single-minded King. He was determined, energetic, and far-sighted, and these qualities were made the more effective by his utter ruthlessness. Though many found him charming, he was faithful only to this three wives.

He came from an aristocratic and politically important family which had its roots in Dalarna. His father and father-in-law were executed by King Christian II of Denmark, along with 80 other prominent Swedes, in Stockholm in 1520. This provoked Gustav Vasa to lead an uprising in Dalarna. Within three years he gained the support of the Hanseatic city of Lübeck and brought his rebellion to a successful conclusion. He was crowned King at Strängnäs in 1523.

By the time of his death, in 1560, he had transformed Sweden. The Germans and the peasants had helped him to defeat the Danes. Then the Danes and the Germans had helped him to smash the peasant rebellions. Later, the nobility and the peasants helped him against the Germans. But his greatest triumph was over the Catholic Church. Nowhere in Europe was the secular character of the early Reformation more pronounced than in Sweden. When the Church, which had originally supported Gustav Vasa, balked at lending him more money, he simply plundered it. Between 1527, when the first taxes were laid on the Church, and 1541, when the first Swedish bible appeared, the power of the Church was utterly broken, and its great wealth—at the start of his reign it owned a fifth of the land in Sweden—shared out between the King and the nobility. An especially unpopular act was the king's seizure of one bell from every parish, for the valuable metal they contained. This somewhat imperious handling of the Church galvanized the peasants into revolt. But to little avail. The King and the nobles broke these rebellions by a mixture of diplomacy and judicious murder.

Gustav Vasa's final triumph was to establish the principle of a hereditary monarchy and he was succeeded by all three of his sons. The elder, Erik XIV, went mad and offended the nobility, who helped his brother Johan III to depose and imprison him. It has not been proved that Johan III was responsible for his brother's death in captivity.

Johan's son, Sigismund, by a Polish princess, became King both of Poland and Sweden. This arrangement suited the Swedish aristocracy, who were left to run the country much as they wanted to while Sigismund was in Poland. This was intolerable to Gustav Vasa's surviving son Karl, the brother of the two previous kings. He raised the peasants against the aristocracy, and triumphed, helped not a little by his nephew Sigismund's vacillations. He took the throne as Karl (or Charles) XI. Throughout this period the new Swedish Kingdom waged a succession of wars in the east in an attempt to control the Gulf of Finland, and in the south against Denmark, where Sweden then reached the Kattegat along a narrow strip south of the Göta river. It was Karl XI who founded the city of Gothenburg to make the most of this strip of land.

Battling for Boundaries

His son, Gustav II Adolf, known to the rest of Europe as Gustavus Adolphus, turned Sweden into the greatest power in northern Europe. He was a general of genius, and his army the most formidable in Europe. It was better drilled, better equipped, and better led than any other. The iron of Bergslagen supplied Sweden with its own armament industry while the peasantry formed the first conscript army in modern Europe. For 14 years Gustav Adolf's armies worked their way along

the Baltic, starting in Finland and slowly moving towards the terrible
Thirty Years' War which devastated Germany between 1618 and 1648.
The Thirty Years' War was religious in origin; it was a religious war,
too, in the unexampled savagery with which it was fought out. But the
political gains for Sweden were immense, though Gustav Adolphus did
not live to see them. He was killed at Lützen in Saxony in 1632. But
the victory he had won in 1631, at Breitenfeld, established Sweden as
a great power.

This seemed at the time to be a triumph of generalship and diplomacy. But it was as much, and probably more, a triumph of the Swedish
state's inward organization, and the rest of Swedish history is largely
a story of domestic change.

The external story is quickly told. Swedish power south of the Baltic
was finally broken at the Battle of Poltava in the Ukraine in 1709. Karl
XII, who was defeated there, was one of the most brilliant soldiers of
his age; brave, skilful, and just that little bit too ambitious. He was
trying to reach Moscow on the Russian campaign that ended in disaster
at Poltava. He survived the battle, and returned via Turkey to Sweden.
When he was killed, probably by his own side, besieging a fortress in
Norway in 1718, it was the end of Sweden's period as an aggressive
power.

A succession of peace treaties followed. The most important was
signed three years after Karl XII was killed, in 1721, with Russia,
which established the present-day boundaries of Finland, and thus
Russia's control of the southern side of the Gulf of Finland, and the
approaches to what was to become St. Petersburg.

The only lasting results of 150 years of nearly continuous war to the
east and in Germany had been the great expansion of Sweden to the
west, where its present boundaries were now fixed at the sea.

Coming of Age

Until Gustav Vasa's reign, Sweden was more a federation of provinces than a country. His always ruthless and occasionally atrocious
crushing of successive peasants' revolts turned Sweden into a national
state, in which class differences supplied the important tensions in
politics, not, as before, in regional differences.

Four classes, or estates, were recognized in Sweden until 1865: the
nobility, the merchants, the peasants, and the clergy. Each estate
formed a distinct part of the Riksdag, which, in the 20th century,
became a parliament. Before then, the Riksdag is perhaps best considered, with the help of a commercial analogy, as the assembled shareholders of Sweden. Naturally, different shares in the country supplied
different voting rights and different privileges. It was definitely advisable to be born into the aristocracy, who not only enjoyed exemption
from many taxes, but also a monopoly on the best jobs in the civil
service. The Riksdag, in its capacity as a "shareholders' meeting," had
the right to approve all taxes. When the succession to the throne was
in doubt, it was the Riksdag which chose a new king (or chief executive), though once a dynasty was established, there was little the Riksdag could do.

The King would be assisted by a Council of State. Sometimes he
chose his own members; sometimes the Riksdag chose them for him.
It all depended on how successful he was, and how well the Riksdag
could imitate the performance of the non-political bureaucracies which

traditionally ran the country on the King's behalf. This was a unique system of government.

In the 18th century, Sweden was preoccupied with internal problems, a period which has been called the Age of Liberty. Constitutional reform, the rise of the party system and constant efforts to limit the power of the king are some of the recurring themes of this era. The Swedish throne was occupied in the last decades of the century by Gustavus III, little known in the outside world except for the fact that he figures as the leading character in Verdi's *Un Ballo in Maschera,* but who created a Golden Age in Swedish culture. Much of the country's rich heritage of architecture, painting, sculpture and theater is due to him and his mother, a dominating sister of Frederick the Great. Gustavus' life was full of highly-colored incidents, his death by assassination not the least of them.

Though Sweden was of course affected by the ideas and wars of the rest of Europe (the turbulence of the Napoleonic Wars caused the loss of Finland to Russia in 1809, and the election of one of Napoleon's Marshals, Count Bernadotte, as the new King of Sweden created a dynasty that still reigns) her politics and ideas have always had a parallel evolution to those of the rest of the world.

The 19th century was a time of great ideological richness and great physical poverty. The technology of Swedish agriculture had hardly changed since the Viking Age. It was quite insufficient to feed a growing population and great numbers of peasant farmers emigrated as a result. And such little Swedish industry as there was had difficulty competing with the technologically advanced and much better capitalized industries of England.

The peasants took refuge from their miseries in evangelical Christianity and teetotalism. While these superstitions did much to give Sweden a largely unjustified reputation for high-minded gloom, they tended also to provide the disciplined workers who were responsible for Sweden's prosperity in this century. The middle classes introduced liberalism to the country: first political liberalism, which brought about the transformation of the Riksdag into a single, elected body, then economic liberalism, which slowly ate at the old guilds and other restraints of trade.

The inheritors of all this were the Social Democrats, who have ruled Sweden, with only a six-year break in the late 1970s, since 1932. They combined, at their best, all the central Swedish traditions: patriotism, hard work, the creation and use of effective bureacracies which could partly create and partly articulate a national consensus.

The Modern Age

Modern Sweden, prosperous, democratic, and neutral, is very largely the creation of the Social Democrats. They would say that it is the creation of the Swedish people; and however irritating it is for an outsider to have the Swedish people identified with only one political party, the claim is almost justified. It has certainly been responsible for the Social Democrats' success.

Perhaps the most remarkable thing they have achieved is to change the constitution of the Swedish people itself. For as far back as history and this essay reaches, the Swedes have been a homogenous nation. They have emigrated to other countries, but immigrants to Sweden have been extremely rare. In the years of unprecedented prosperity after World War II, all this changed. Immigrants flooded into Sweden, mostly from Finland, but also from southern Europe, and—as political refugees—from all over the world. Every eighth child growing up in Sweden now is of immigrant descent. But this unprecedented transformation of society has been accomplished entirely peacefully, and to the benefit of all the groups involved. It is a remarkable tribute to Swedish society that the country's history should have culminated in this peaceful and satisfying way.

SWEDISH FOOD AND DRINK

Of Smörgåsbord and Sill

It is the forests, in their dual roles as providers of food and barriers to commerce, that have shaped Swedish cooking. Only in the broad, fertile plains of Skåne, historically a part of Denmark rather than Sweden, will you come across a more Germanic, northern European style of cooking, full of rich geese and eels.

The forests—perhaps one should say "the forest" since it extends unbroken for perhaps 1,000 miles northwards from Skåne to Lapland —provide an extraordinary abundance of food such as berries, mush-rooms and game. And through the forests wind the river routes, and the fish of these rivers are the third feature of Swedish cooking.

The Swedes eat fish that the Anglo-Saxons would never bother with: and the loss is ours. The obvious fish are there in quantity. The coastal rivers once abounded in salmon, while trout, char and grayling are all common in the north. Perch and northern pike can be caught all year round, and are cooked with skill and relish by the Swedes. Most of these fish are poached and, indeed, butter is seldom used in traditional Swedish cooking, being replaced, for frying purposes, by lard; and any fish is better poached than fried in lard. Yet one of the few truly great Swedish recipes involves no cooking at all. This is *gravad* fish—a method of pickling salmon or trout using salt, sugar, and dill weed. The method is not always successful. But when it is well done the result is superb: more interesting and more delicate than any other salmon dish.

Gravad Lax, as this salmon dish is called, seems at the moment to be becoming fashionable (and very expensive) abroad. It is still worth seeking out in Sweden, for this is the country where it is done best.

The Tale of the Herring

No single dish of herring is quite as good as *gravad lax,* yet there is no doubt that the herring is the most important fish in Swedish cooking. The Swedes eat herring at Christmas and at midsummer; and at all times in between. They fry them and they bake them and they grill them. They pickle them in innumerable ways. In the north they ferment them till perfectly rotten, then eat them with great gusto. This last dish, *surströmming,* requires a strong stomach, and an insensitive nose. An iron liver helps too, since it must be washed down with heroic draughts of schnapps. There is a theory current in the south of the country as to why northerners eat *surströmming:* the smell keeps away people who might otherwise share the bottle.

In fact, the dish is a survival from the days when food could be preserved only with difficulty. Great barrels of *surströmming* accompanied the armies of Gustavus Adolphus in the Thirty Years' War. Indeed the necessity of preserving food is one of the constraints that has shaped Swedish cooking. For though the Swedish countryside has periods of great abundance, there is certainly nothing to be had from it during the winter that lasts for anything from three to eight months.

More conventionally pickled herring, known as *sill,* can be delicious. There are so many varieties that one cannot say with confidence that "*sill* is wonderful," any more than one could say "cheese is marvelous," or "sausages are." It all depends on which cheese, and which sausage—and which *sill.* And in none of those cases is there any reliable guide other than tasting as many varieties as you can, and deciding which you like. Having said that, there is one Swedish cheese at least that no one should miss: *Västerbotten.* The original sin of Swedish cheese, from which few ever redeem themselves, is blandness. The porous, off-white, faintly salted substance sold in red, wax-covered spheres as *Hushållsost* (household cheese) defies comparison except with the equally mysterious, hard yellow stuff known in Britain solely as "cheese." But *Västerbotten* cheese is a delight: and one of the few Swedish cheeses that should properly be eaten at the end of a feast, and not at the beginning, with the herring.

A Swedish Feast

The feast in question is, of course, a *Smörgåsbord,* and the essential think about a *Smörgåsbord* is that it is a feast for a special occasion. It is no more typical of Swedish cooking than the guards outside Buckingham Palace are of the British Army. Though I have worked through numerous grisly banquets at Swedish celebrations, I have never come across a *Smörgåsbord* in a private home, though everyone feels obliged to produce the smaller Christmas feast, that usually centers round a ham.

The *Smörgåsbord* needs to be approached with reverence, a full wallet, and an empty stomach. For everyday eating, one does better to concentrate on single dishes, just as the Swedes do, for the *Smörgåsbord,* too, can be seen as a product of the forests, and of the rhythm of life they impose. Once or twice a year whole villages might gather to celebrate something, but for the most part, each homestead ate by itself. Many of the old dishes have been forgotten now—they require too much time to prepare in an age of TV dinners—or, like spiced meatballs, they survive in a degenerate, frozen form, but are still very good when properly made. Others, like *ärtsoppa,* a thick soup made with peas and pork, are among the most delicious peasant foods of Europe.

Another characteristic of Swedish cooking is the use of unconventional sauces and flavorings. *Ärtsoppa* is eaten with sweet, coarse-grained mustard; meatballs can be eaten with jam made of berries. Pancakes, the quintessential food of a Swedish summer, are also eaten with jelly and sometimes even with soup. All these things are worth trying.

The background to all these goods is the potato. I sometimes wonder what Swedes ate before the potato was introduced from America. There must be some answer: turnips, or birch bark (which was actually made into bread in times of famine). But human life, as we now know it in Sweden, is unthinkable without potatoes. Boiled new potatoes to celebrate midsummer; slightly older potatoes to eat with boiled crayfish by moonlight in August; salads of chopped potato, herring, and beetroot at Christmas time; a *gratin* of potatoes, cream, and anchovies (the famous *Janssöns Frestelse*) on winter evenings: spiced mashed potatoes sold with sausages as a snack in every market place. It is possible, after some time of this, to develop a yearning for pasta.

Mother's Ruin

Potatoes and grains are also responsible for the great Swedish drink of vodka. Swedish beer, alas, is for the most part dreadful. Pale, sweetish, and gassy, it can only be choked down chilled, and appears to have been brewed by militant teetotallers. But the various Swedish vodkas are for the most part correspondingly good. Many are flavored with herbs, and it would be an amusing enterprise for a millionaire to sample each one of the forty or so kinds on sale.

For, like all Swedish drink, vodka is expensive and difficult to get at. Only the very rich or foolhardy drink spirits in restaurants, though beer is more or less affordable. The best bargain available for the tourist is undoubtedly wine. The Swedish State Alcohol Monopoly, which dispenses its wares through gloomy shops known as "Systembolags," is the largest single purchaser of wine in the world; and it buys wisely. Wine is no more expensive in Sweden than it is in the United States or England. Good wine may even be slightly cheaper. Anyone traveling on a budget through Sweden would be wise to drink wine only at picnics; this wisdom could be richly rewarded.

But, then, anyone who has traveled through Sweden on a budget will wonder what all the preceding chapter has been about. For, if one is to judge by what is available in the cheaper restaurants, then the principal food of Sweden is pizza.

STOCKHOLM

Open Nature and City Planning

Stockholm, Sweden's capital, has been called the most beautiful city in the world. This is open to debate, but few will deny that it is a handsome and civilized capital with a natural setting that would be hard to beat anywhere. When it was founded as a fortress on a little stone island where Lake Mälar reaches the Baltic, nobody cared much about natural beauty. It was protection the founders were after, military defense. But around the year 1250, the fortress became a town, and the town, spreading to nearby islands and finally to the mainland, became a city. And, though Nature remained the same, men's opinion of it changed, and Stockholm delights the tourist today with its openness, its space, its vistas over a great expanse of water. Of course it's been called the "Venice of the North," but that happens sooner or later to any northern city with more water than can be supplied by a fire hydrant.

Stockholm's beauty has been jealously guarded by the city fathers. The town is full of parks, tree-lined squares and boulevards, playgrounds, wading pools and other amenities of urban life, and the building codes are extremely strict. Nature and city planning have thus combined to create a pleasing metropolis, and it is hard to realize as you gaze out over the water from a table on the Strömparterren terrace that you are in the heart of a bustling metropolis, a town that has grown from less than 100,000 inhabitants to over a million in the space of a century.

Nowhere is the striking modernity of much of Stockholm more obvious than in the brand new streets and squares around Sergels Torg, a startling glass and steel tower in the heart of the new city, and the rail station, where multi-lane highways, skyscrapers and underground shopping malls have all sprung up in the space of a few years. Yet no more than five minutes' walk will bring you to the medieval heart of the city on the islands of Gamla Stan (Old Town), where narrow twisting streets huddle around the bulk of the imposing Royal Palace, the Cathedral and the Riksdag, the Parliament.

June, July and August are the best months to visit this capital. Then you have the best weather and the greatest variety of sight-seeing facilities. Bring a reasonably warm coat along. What most people would call a mild summer day is apt to be announced in the Stockholm papers as a heat wave. In May or October the weather is brisker, but so is the normal life of Stockholm.

History and Growth

The earliest origins of Stockholm are largely unknown. Perhaps the first somewhat reliable report is a Viking saga, which, as all Viking sagas should, ends in violence. It seems that Agne, a warrior king of the Ynglinga dynasty, had been off on a visit to Finland. There, among other treasures, he had acquired a chieftain's daughter named Skjalf, by the effective if crude device of cutting down her father. Coming home, he stopped on the shore of an island which is now a part of Stockholm, to drink the health of his new bride and a proper toast to his late father-in-law. The mead flowed freely, Agne slept, Skjalf freed her fellow Finnish prisoners, and they hanged Agne. Then the Finns safely sailed home. The place was subsequently called Agnefit, or Agne Strand.

The first written mention of Stockholm in preserved chronicles gives the date 1252. Tradition—and some historical evidence—has it that a powerful regent named Birger Jarl here founded a fortified castle and city, locking off the entrance to Lake Mälar and the region around it. At all events, it is known that a castle of substance was built in the 13th century, and during the same period the Great Church was begun (dedicated to St. Nicholas, patron saint of shipping) and the first monasteries.

From these dim beginnings the history of the city can be divided into four fairly distinct epochs: the erratic, confused first centuries; the arrival of King Gustav Vasa, who made Stockholm a capital beginning in 1523; King Gustavus Adolphus, who made it the heart of an empire a century later; and the modern era.

After the time of Birger Jarl the Swedish nation, still unorganized, groped its way forward. Up to this time Stockholm had not been the capital; the latest city to enjoy the favor had been Sigtuna. The real physical heart of Sweden remained uncertain. Nevertheless, Magnus Eriksson, a king of some importance, was crowned here in 1336. Toward the end of the century Sweden, Norway, and Denmark were united under one ruler. A period of confusion and revolt followed. Stockholm continued to be a commercial center, with monopoly trading rights for much of the territory around.

On Midsummer's Eve, 1523, when King Gustav Vasa returned from his victorious uprising for Swedish independence from the union (and from a Danish king), the real history of Stockholm began. Vasa was a powerful figure, sometimes called the George Washington of Sweden, and, although he moved from castle to castle throughout the country, his treasure chamber was in the old Stockholm Royal Palace. Succeeding kings tended in the same direction, making Stockholm more and more important.

Under Gustavus Adolphus, a great organizer as well as a military leader, who reigned from 1611 to 1632, the city became a capital in fact as well as name. Sweden had already begun to engage in political machinations and wars on the Continent and in Russia. It was partly his need to keep his military forces at top efficiency, his need for tax money, for supplies and for men that led Gustavus to concentrate the administration of the country in Stockholm. When he died on the battlefield of Lützen in 1632, Protestantism had been saved, Sweden had become an empire and Stockholm was its capital.

Prosperity and population grew accordingly. Gustavus himself, in a farewell address of 1630, had told the citizens of Sweden's cities that he hoped "your small cottages may become large stone houses". Many of them did. From a population of perhaps 3,000 when Gustav Vasa came home victorious, the number of inhabitants had grown to some 9,000 by the time Gustavus Adolphus fell, and rose to perhaps 35,000 by 1660. Meanwhile, the wars continued. Fortunately for Stockholm, they were fought on foreign soil. This did not, however, diminish the importance of the city, for it functioned as the capital even during the long absence of hero King Charles XII, who spent almost his entire reign in the field—losing much of what Gustavus Adolphus had won.

Rulers came and went, political battles were fought, won, and lost. But the building of Stockholm went on, sometimes in the hands of eminent architects like Nicodemus Tessin and his son, who are responsible for both the Royal Palace and Drottningholm Palace, as well as many other buildings which still stand. In the 18th century, Stockholm began to attract scientists and scholars, to share the spotlight with Lund and Uppsala as a center of learning. Gustav III (assassinated in 1792), a dilettante who could put on steel gauntlets when required, did much to make Stockholm a cultural, musical, and dramatic capital.

In 1850 Stockholm was still a quiet town. It had many of the stately buildings which even now give it its characteristic profile, but it numbered less than 100,000 people—a peaceful administrative center, perhaps dreaming of past glories. The first municipal cleaning department was established in 1859, the first waterworks in 1861, and gaslights had arrived but a few years earlier. As late as 1860, Drottninggatan, the most prominent commercial street, had no sidewalks. But the same year the first train arrived from Södertälje, 25 miles away. Modern communications had been born. The new era had begun.

Modern Development

The last 100 years of Stockholm's history are the story of a peaceful revolution, of industrialization, and of the remaking of a government from a monarchy with four estates in the parliament—nobles, clergy, farmers, as well as burghers—into a full parliamentary democracy with a king at its head. As the country has progressed and grown, Stockholm has progressed and grown with it. You will see the physical evidence wherever you go—the squat Parliament House on the site of one-time royal stables; the City Hall, a splendidly quirky and lavish brick creation overlooking the waters of Lake Mälar; the extensive and striking developments in the center of the city; and two huge satellite suburbs to the west and east of the city.

Exploring Stockholm

If Stockholm's island geography poses communication problems, it has the advantage of dividing the city neatly into sections and of making it possible to know easily where you are.

Gamla Stan. The Old Town, site of the Royal Palace and center of the city and nation, and the adjoining islands, Riddarholmen (The Isle of Knights), and Helgeandsholmen (Island of the Holy Spirit).

Södermalm. As the name implies, this is the southern section, across the bridge leading from the Old Town.

Norrmalm. North of the Old Town, the financial and business heart of the city. The new building construction from Hötorget to Klarabergsgatan, which forms the new commercial center of Stockholm, constitutes the most important part of the redevelopment of Nedre Norrmalm (Lower Norrmalm).

Kungsholmen. A large island west of Norrmalm, site of the Town Hall, and most of the offices of the city government.

Östermalm. East of Norrmalm, largely residential, many embassies and consulates.

Djurgården. The huge island which is mostly park, projecting east toward the Baltic Sea in the channels between Östermalm and Södermalm. Here are concentrated museums, including Skansen, the openair museum, amusement parks, restaurants.

Regardless of how long you intend to stay and how thoroughly you expect to see the city, begin by one or more boat excursions. Nothing else can give you a quick idea of the unique nature of Stockholm.

Let's take as a starting point the south of the large downtown park known as the Royal Gardens (Kungsträdgården), just across the rushing channel from the Royal Palace. It's an ummistakable point, easy to find. Immediately beside you is the striking profile of the statue of King Charles XII, arm raised and pointing east; behind him stretches the long park; to his right the unmistakable solid stone of the Royal Opera House, a block or so to his left the familiar façade of the Grand Hotel; and across the water the dominating walls of the palace. Furthermore, just at the water's edge at both sides of the bridge there are kiosks that serve as starting points for some of the boat and bus excursions which show you the city.

The best way to see the city is by boat—there is practically no major place of interest in and around Stockholm that isn't within easy reach of the many little boats that ply around the busy harbor. But you'll find it equally easy to explore the city on foot. Most of the principal sights are concentrated in the center of Stockholm and are relatively close to one another. If you feel like venturing further afield, use the excellent subway system, the T-banan; many of the stations are carved from solid rock, creating an eerie, grotto-like atmosphere.

Gamla Stan

The best place to begin your exploration of the city is the Old Town, Gamla Stan, situated on three little islands. From the statue of Charles XII at the foot of the Kungsträdgården, there are two bridges leading to the Old Town, both no more than a couple of minutes' walk away.

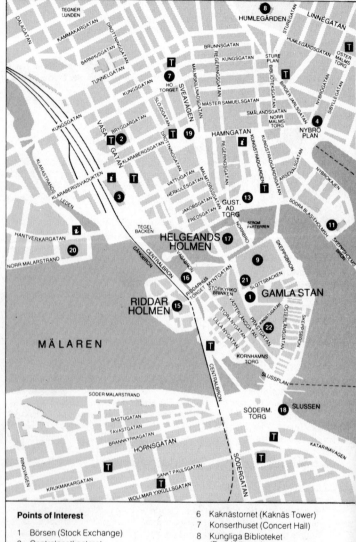

Points of Interest

1 Börsen (Stock Exchange)

2 Centralpostkontoret
(Central Post Office)

3 Central Rail Station

4 Dramatiska Teatern
(Royal Dramatic Theater)

5 Historiska Museet (Museum of
National Antiquities)

6 Kaknästornet (Kaknäs Tower)

7 Konserthuset (Concert Hall)

8 Kungliga Biblioteket
(Royal Library)

9 Kungliga Slottet (Royal Palace);
Livrustkammaren (Royal Armory)

10 Moderna Museet (Museum of
Modern Art)

11 Nationalmuseet
(National Museum)

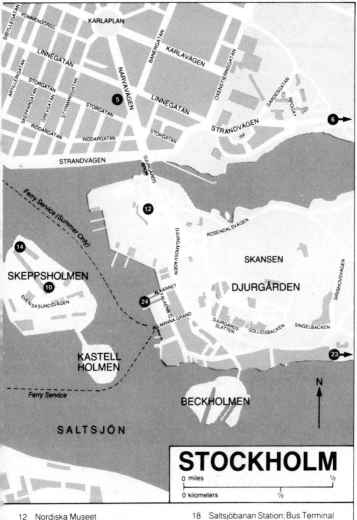

STOCKHOLM

0 miles ½

0 kilometers ½

12	Nordiska Museet (Nordic Museum)	18	Saltsjöbanan Station; Bus Terminal
13	Operan (Royal Opera House)	19	Sergels Torg
14	Östasiatiska Museet (Museum of Far Eastern Antiquities)	20	Stadshuset (Town Hall)
15	Riddarholmskyrkan (Riddarholm Church)	21	Storkyrkan (Cathedral)
16	Riddarhuset (House of Nobility); Supreme Court	22	Tyska Kyrkan (German Church)
17	Riksdag (Parliament)	23	Waldemarsudde
		24	Wasavarvet (Wasa Museum)
		T	Subway Stations
		i	Tourist Information Offices

The more interesting, however, is the second, the Norrbro, leading directly to the imposing bulk of the Royal Palace. As you cross the bridge, you'll also see the Parliament building, a ponderous stone structure dating from the turn of the century, on your right. And just behind and to one side of the Parliament building is the one-time building of the Bank of Sweden, the oldest existing bank in the world, founded in 1656. Today the building is used as offices for members of parliament.

The Royal Palace is not old, as palaces go, but the site is. It was here that Stockholm was born. The original palace, the Three Crowns, burned down one night in 1697, with the exception of the northern wing of today's palace. A new palace on the old site was ordered immediately. Three generations of Sweden's most famous architectural dynasty had an important part in its creation—Nicodemus Tessin the Elder planned the exterior and began the interior decoration, which was continued by his son, Tessin the Younger, and grandson, Carl Gustav Tessin. The whole project took more than 60 years, and was not completed until 1760. The building consists basically of a perfect square—enclosing a large court—with two wings sticking out on the east side and another on the west.

A number of interiors are open to the public. You may be interested in the Hall of State, which contains the king's silver throne. The Chapel Royal in the same wing has, among other impressive historical and artistic treasures, pews saved from the old palace. If you have time, look in on the Apartments of State, the Apartments of King Oscar II and Queen Sophie, and the Guest Apartments, notable for the furnishings and extremely fine Gobelin tapestries. There's also a palace museum, with bits of the previous palace, other historical finds, and the collection of classical sculpture brought from Italy by King Gustav III in the 1780s. The Royal Treasury, in the old vaults, can now be visited.

Diagonally across the street from the south side of the palace, and intimately associated with it, is the Great Church, the Stockholm cathedral and, in a sense, the national church. You would hardly guess from the well-kept exterior that it is believed to be the oldest building in the city, dating from about 1250. Many Swedish kings have been crowned here (until Gustav V gave up the custom when he ascended the throne in 1907), and it is still used for solemn celebrations attended by the king. There are a number of art treasures, of which perhaps the oldest, best known, and most distinguished is the statue carved in wood of St. George and the Dragon by Bernt Notke of Lübeck, which was presented to the church in 1489 to commemorate a Swedish victory over the Danes some 18 years earlier. A sound and light show is performed here for a few weeks during summer.

You are in the heart of the Old Town now and there are several ways of continuing your look about. Here are two good suggestions immediately at hand. The first is to walk downhill on the lane called Storkyrkobrinken, to the right of the main entrance of the Great Church as you come out. This lane, like practically all those of the Old Town, follows the same route it did in the Middle Ages. Everywhere around you are buildings centuries old, living history. At the base of the hill you step out in a little square called Riddarhustorget. The two dominating buildings, across the square from where you enter, both date from the 17th century. One is Riddarhuset, House of the Nobility, in which you will find the crests of Swedish noble families. The white palace to its right was once a private possession, became the city courthouse in the 18th century, and is now occupied by the Supreme Court.

From here you will see the weathered red brick and openwork spire of Riddarholm Church. This is the Swedish Pantheon, burial place of Swedish kings for about four centuries. The most famous figures buried here are King Gustavus Adolphus, hero of the Thirty Years' War, and Charles XII (in Swedish, Karl XII), who is renowned for his signal victories over the Russian and Continental armies, with inferior forces, until the tide turned against him and he fell in Norway in 1718. Two medieval kings, Magnus Ladulås, who died in 1290, and Karl Knutson Bonde, some 180 years later, are also buried here. The latest king to be put to rest was Gustav V, on November 9, 1950. Except for the funeral of a king, the church has not been used for services for a long time. The sarcophagi of the various rulers, usually embellished with their monograms, are clearly visible in the small chapels given over to the various dynasties. The church building itself is interesting as the second oldest structure in Stockholm. It is a former monastery church completed about 1290, with many additions since.

Take five minutes to continue past the church down to the quay on Lake Mälar. It's well worth it. You get a fine view of the lake, the magnificent arches of the West Bridge in the distance, the southern heights, and above all the imposing profile of the Town Hall, which appears to be almost floating on the water. At the quay you may see one of the Göta Canal ships.

The second alternative to continuing your stroll from the Great Church is to turn left as you come out of the main entrance and walk up Trångsund to a little square called Stortorget, the oldest square in Stockholm. The dominating building, on the north side, is the Stock Exchange. This is also the headquarters of the Swedish Academy, which awards the Nobel Prize in literature. The other buildings are also old; note the tall, narrow, red merchant house and its sculptured portal from the 17th century.

The Old Town is the perfect kind of place to wander around without any decided aim, looking at the old portals, poking about in crowded antique shops, savoring the Bohemian atmosphere and the sense of age, peeking into doll-sized courtyards, making your way through curving, narrow lanes. There is little auto traffic, and the passages are too narrow to provide both streets and sidewalks. Go along Skomakarega-tan to the German Church (Tyska Kyrkan), turn right for a few meters, then left again on Prästgatan. Keep your eyes open as you near the end of Prästgatan, on the right you will see one of the narrowest thorough-fares in the world. It is called Mårten Trotzigs Gränd (*gränd* means lane), and leads down to Västerlånggatan. It is scarcely a meter wide, half of it is a stairway, yet it is a public thoroughfare maintained and lighted by the city.

It's only a couple of short blocks from here to the south end of the Old Town. You should really stroll on to that point. Above you are the southern heights, connected with the Old Town by an intricate clover-leaf of bridges and streets at about four levels, called Slussen. Katarina elevator—you see it poking up all by itself on the other side of the channel—takes you up to a platform with a fine view of Stockholm.

Though the Old Town is, of course, the most ancient and historic part of the city, you will have noticed by now that it is by no means lacking in modern chic. In fact it is very definitely the trendiest area of the city, both for shopping and eating, with a veritable surfeit of expensive and glamorous restaurants and shops: there are some 300 restaurants alone.

Skansen

After the sophistication and history of the Old Town, the openair amusement park of Skansen, founded in 1891, provides a striking contrast. It is situated on the large island of Djurgården, located to the east of the city. The park contains a museum, a zoo, numerous restaurants and cafes, a circus, an aquarium, a theater, a concert hall and much else besides, all combining to make it one of the enduring highlights of the city. One of its principal delights are the buildings—farm houses, windmills, barns, whole estates almost—that have been brought here from all parts of the country, giving even the most casual visitor a taste of traditional rural Sweden. There is even an 18th-century church that is still used for divine services and weddings. But many of the other buildings are in use too. Geese cackle near the entrance to the farm houses from southern Sweden; glass blowers blow glass—you can help blow it if you want to—in the old-time glass blower's hut.

Here also are moose, wolves, foxes and other Nordic animals; Sweden's largest aquarium with Cuban crocodiles; and nocturnal bushbabies, pygmy kangaroos and other strange animals in the Moonlight Hall. Many activities designed especially for children include a children's zoo.

You can walk to Skansen from the statue of Charles XII in about 30 minutes. It is a long walk, but it will take you through much of Stockholm's most gracious and substantial waterfront areas, past elegant apartment blocks and smart shops, with yachts and ferry boats ever-present, particularly on the broad expanse of Strandvägen.

Djurgården is also home to three outstanding museums: the Nordiska Museum, the Waldemarsudde and the *Wasa*. The *Wasa* is the most popular of the three, and for good reasons. The museum, distinguished by a blocky cantilevered exterior, contains one of the most remarkable maritime exhibits in the world—the 17th-century warship *Wasa,* once the pride of the Swedish navy, built at vast expense and the most powerful fighting ship of her day in the Baltic. Launched amid great pomp, she set out on her maiden voyage on August 10, 1628 in full view of the population of Stockholm, including of course the King himself. She had sailed less than a mile when a gust caught her, and she heeled over and unceremoniously sank—the *Titanic* of her day. Her precious guns were immediately salvaged, but with the passage of time the *Wasa* faded from memory.

However, in 1956 her position was rediscovered and it was found that, remarkably, the briny waters of the harbor had all but preserved her intact. A complex and difficult salvage operation was begun and in May 1961 the *Wasa* was raised to the surface and moved to her present location. Painstaking restoration has returned the ship almost to her original condition, providing the visitor with an unparalled experience of life afloat in a great warship of the past: regular guided tours, an interesting film (with English sub-titles) and a small attached museum help bring the ship to vibrant life. There are plans to move the ship to a new site a few hundred meters away by 1990, but even in her present cramped home she provides a magnificent experience.

The Nordiska Museum (the Nordic Museum), housed in a splendid late-Victorian pile, is located just by the Djurgårdsbron, the bridge leading to Djurgården. It contains a vast collection of exhibits that chart Sweden's progress from 1500. Of particular interest are some magnificent fabrics, costumes and rugs, a lovely collection of bridal gowns and the charming gold and silver coronets traditionally worn by Swedish brides.

Finally, visit Prince Eugen's "Waldemarsudde," the former home of "the Painter Prince," brother of the late King Gustav V, which was bequeathed to the people on the prince's death. The many paintings, some by Eugen himself, constitute a fine collection of Swedish art, and the mansion, art gallery, and beautiful grounds are well worth seeing.

Treasures of the Town Hall

The Stockholm Town Hall, one of the great architectural works of the 20th century, is another appropriate excursion that you can manage in a couple of hours—more if you like. Starting at the statue of Charles XII, turn to the right and merely follow the waterfront until you arrive at its massive portal. The distance is less than a couple of kilometers.

Superlatives have not been lacking in describing the structure. It has sometimes been called "the most beautiful building of this century in Europe." This opinion is not unanimous, of course; some people have reacted violently against it, but even this sharp reaction is a measure of the strength of the total impression. The building was completed and dedicated in 1923, and has become a symbol of the city. It is the seat of the city council and central administration.

The building is certainly unusual—a massive square tower rising from the corner of a graceful central block, the whole built of dark and delicately worked brick and topped by pale-green roofs with spires, domes and minarets abounding. It successfully synthesizes elements of traditional Swedish architecture, notably in the tower, which is derived from the massive castles of 16th-century Sweden, with classical elements, the resulting mixture spiced by Oriental and Byzantine windows and spires. It is difficult to decide finally whether the end-product is beautiful or kitsch—it is undoubtedly impressive.

You can go inside and look around. Among the highlights are the Golden Hall, whose walls are decorated lavishly with mosaics; the Blue Hall, confusingly named perhaps, as the only blue visible is the sky glimpsed through the windows ranged around the top of the walls; and the Prince's Gallery, with large murals by Prince Eugene. You can also go up the 106-meter (348-foot) tower (don't worry, there's an elevator) for a predictably spectacular view. At noon and 6 P.M. the carillon plays the medieval war song of the Swedes that helped gird their loins at the Battle of Brunkeberg in 1471. The adjoining Maiden Tower is surmounted by a bronze St. George and the Dragon. Finally, visit the Terrace, a formal garden on the banks of Lake Mälar with wonderful views of the Old Town and the southern heights rising beyond it.

Other Sights

Depending on the amount of time you have available and your special interests, there are many other places and institutions well worth a visit. Among the dozens of museums, these are particularly recommended: The National Museum, just a few doors down the quay from the Grand Hotel, which is home to the largest collection of paintings and sculptures, by both Swedish and foreign artists, in the country.

A few minutes' walk from here on the island of Skeppsholmen are the Museum of Modern Art and the Museum of Far Eastern Antiquities, both with fine collections, the latter a pleasing spot to explore or simply from which to admire the view of the Old Town.

The National Museum of Antiquities and Royal Cabinet of Coins, located to the east of the city on the spacious boulevard of Narvavägen, contains a veritable mass of historical finds dating back well into the Stone Age.

Although not a museum, there is a further attraction on Djurgården—the 155-meter (508-foot) high Kaknäs Tower. The fastest elevators in Europe hurtle you up to the observation deck, from where an unparalleled view of the city and the Stockholm Archipelago stretches before you.

Music and Markets

The Concert Hall, at Hötorget, is the center of Stockholm's musical life. The building, designed by Ivar Tengbom, was completed in 1926. In front is Carl Milles' huge sculptured group of Orpheus calling up the spirits. It is in this hall that the awarding of the Nobel Prizes takes place.

It's well worth your while to get to one of the market squares fairly early in the day—9:00 A.M. will do—which are masses of color whatever the season of the year. One is just in front of the Concert House, another on Östermalm. Flowers, fresh fruits and vegetables are the principal stock in trade. Look in at the indoor markets which adjoin these squares—there you can fill your whole grocery basket from the little shops of independent dealers, and have a snack in one of the small restaurants. This is a unique aspect of Stockholm life. Incidentally, the outdoor markets operate right through the winter.

Excursions from Stockholm

Immediately outside the city limits of Stockholm proper are a number of popular attractions which you can reach within an hour by public transportation, or half an hour by car.

The sculptor Carl Milles, who was perhaps better known as an inhabitant of Cranbrook, Michigan, had his permanent home on the island of Lidingö, a Stockholm suburb, where he collected not only some of his own works, but also other outstanding pieces from several eras and countries. It was here at Millesgården that he died in September 1955, still hard at work at the age of 80, and the collection is now open to the public daily from March through December.

The royal palace of Drottningholm is located on a little island in Lake Mälar—the name means "Queen's Island"—a few kilometers from Stockholm. The trip is a pleasant experience, particularly by boat. If you have seen Versailles, you will be reminded of it at once when you arrive at Drottningholm, for it was clearly inspired by the French style. The palace was built by Nicodemus Tessin the Elder, and his son, Tessin the Younger, completed the gardens in the style of Le Nôtre.

Drottningholm is one of the most delightful of European palaces, embracing, as it does, all that was best in the art of living practiced by mid-18th-century royalty. In the grounds, a kind of Trianon, is the China Palace, conceived in Chinoiserie terms, a lovely little palace, hidden in the trees, where the royal family could relax and entertain

STOCKHOLM 43

their friends. Also in the grounds is the Theater. This fascinating building slumbered like the Sleeping Beauty undisturbed for well over a century, the settings and stage machinery of the 18th century in perfect condition and working order. It now houses a theater museum and delightful productions of baroque opera are once again staged in the auditorium that saw the efforts of Gustavus III to create a Swedish Golden Age. The Royal Family occupies one wing at the palace.

Haga Palace, formerly the home of the late Crown Prince Gustav Adolf, is located only a few minutes from downtown, right on the city limits of Stockholm. A more interesting building located on the same grounds is Haga Pavilion. It is a miniature summer palace built by Gustav III (late 18th century), exquisitely furnished.

The resort of Saltsjöbaden is a residential suburb the year round. During the summer it is a rendezvous for yachtsmen and motorboat enthusiasts, and the harbor is excellent. In winter there is skating, skate-sailing, iceboating, and skiing. The modern Stockholm observatory is located here. You can reach Saltsjöbaden from Slussen on an electric train. In the same general direction, but to the north, is Gustavsberg, where the noted ceramics works may be visited in groups by previous appointment.

PRACTICAL INFORMATION FOR STOCKHOLM

GETTING TO TOWN FROM THE AIRPORT. Buses from Arlanda Airport to the city, a distance of 45 km. (28 miles) are frequent. The trip takes about 40 minutes and the bus stops at Ulriksdal and at the Haga Air Terminal. The final stop is at the Central Station in the center of town. The Sheraton, Royal Viking, Terminus and Continental hotels are all within two minutes' walk. The fare is approximately SEK 40, payable to the driver. You can also buy a ticket at special ticket offices at the airport and the air terminal. A scheduled bus service to Brommaplan from the airport is also available, with stops at Kista and Sundbyberg subway stations.

A taxi to the city from the airport will cost you about SEK 350. However, SAS Scandinavian Airlines operates a limousine service on a shared-taxi basis, which takes you direct to your hotel or any other address in the Greater Stockholm area for about SEK 165 or 210 according to distance. The limousine can be booked on arrival at Arlanda Airport; for the return journey ask your hotel to make a reservation well in advance—the previous day, if possible. If two or more passengers take the limousine to the same address, only the first pays the full fare; the others pay 50%.

TOURIST INFORMATION. The Tourist Center is located in the middle of the city in Sverigehuset (Sweden House), opposite the large department store *Nordiska Kompaniet,* or *N.K.,* in Kungsträdgården (789 20 00). There you will find information about interesting sights and events, one-day tours and so on and you can make bookings for sightseeing excursions. It also sells maps, postcards, books and souvenirs. The Tourist Center is open every day.

A useful publications is *Stockholm This Week* which you can get from most hotels and all tourist centers. From a kiosk on Norrmalmstorg you can buy last-minute tickets at reduced prices to concerts and theaters. (Tickets can also be bought at most post offices and at the Media Center in Gallerian).

USEFUL ADDRESSES. Embassies. *American Embassy,* Strandvägen 101 (783 53 00). *British Embassy,* Skarpögatan 6–8 (67 01 40). *Canadian Embassy,* Tegelbacken 4 (near the Sheraton) (23 79 20).

Travel Agents. *American Express,* Birger Jarlsgatan 1 (23 53 30). *Cooks,* Vasagatan 22 (762 58 27).

Car-Hire. *Avis,* Albygatan 109B, 171 54 Solna (29 09 09); *Bonus Biluthyrning,* Östgötagatan 75 (41 09 09); *Esso,* Box 5833 (63 92 82); *Europcar,* Birger Jarlsgatan (23 10 70); *Hertz,* Mäster Samuelsgatan 67B (24 07 20); *InterRent,* Hotel Sheraton, Tegelbacken 6 (21 06 50). All the major car-hire companies also have desks at Arlanda Airport.

TELEPHONE CODES. The telephone code for Stockholm is 08. To call any number in this chapter, unless otherwise specified, this prefix must be used. Within the city, no prefix is required.

HOTELS. It is recommended that you reserve hotel rooms well in advance, especially from September to November. If you arrive in Stockholm without a reservation, consult the Hotellcentralen in the underground Central Station. This room-booking service is open daily 8 A.M.—9P.M. June through Sept. For the rest of the year it is open Mon. to Fri. 8.30–5, and, in May only, Sat. 8–5, Sun. 1–9. A charge is made for each room reserved. Most hotels have smoke-free rooms and rooms for the handicapped. Breakfast is usually included in the room rate. In general, Stockholm hotels are comfortable, but prices are fairly high.

For information about low-priced packages at weekends and daily during the summer months, write to *Destination Stockholm,* Stora Hoparegränd 5, S-11130 Stockholm (14 09 00). This company offers Stockholm packages which include low hotel rates, free transportation within the city and free or reduced entry to museums. Travelers with caravans can make arrangements to park them at some schools in the city during the summer months. Enquire at tourist offices.

Deluxe

Amaranten. Kungsholmsgatan 31 (54 10 60). 415 rooms. Contains the *Amaryllis* restaurant, the *Travellers'* piano bar and a nightclub called *Cindy.* It also boasts a Japanese-style recreation area and an "executive tower" with a roof garden and luxurious accommodation. (SARA) AE, DC, MC, V.

Anglais. Humlegårdsgatan 23 (24 99 00). 211 rooms. One of the leading hotels in Stockholm, conveniently situated near shopping districts and the subway. Popular restaurant, own video channel, garage. (RESO). AE, DC, MC, V.

Clas på Hörnet. Surbrunnsgatan 20 (16 51 30). 10 rooms. Arguably the most exclusive hotel in Stockholm, in an elegant 200-year-old town house. Excellent restaurant. AE, DC, MC, V.

Grand. Blasieholmshamnen 8 (22 10 20). 350 rooms; front rooms face the Royal Palace and the waterfront. A distinguished European deluxe hotel. SAS office, splendid ballroom, famous restaurant. *Thé dansant* on Sun. AE, DC, MC, V.

Grand Hotel Saltsjöbaden. Saltsjöbaden (717 00 20). 103 rooms in a suburban resort setting, 30 minutes by train from Slussen. Castle-like building in landscaped grounds fronting on to the water, with a marina. Restaurant with a wonderful view. Sauna. AE, DC, MC, V.

Mälardrottningen (Queen of Lake Mälar). Riddarholmen (24 36 00). 59 cabins on what was formerly American heiress—and wife of Cary Grant—Barbara Hutton's luxury yacht (built 1924). All cabins are furnished to deluxe hotel standards and the yacht has an attractive permanent berth at Riddarholmskajen, close to the Old Town. It has a restaurant and a bar on the bridge. AE, DC, MC, V.

Royal Viking. Vasagatan 1 (14 10 00). 390 rooms. The newest hotel of high international standard. Within walking distance of the city center and shopping. Has a "skybar" overlooking the Town Hall and Old Town, a relaxation center with saunas (private saunas also available) and a wintergarden, the *Royal Atrium*, with a 36-meter-high (120-ft.) ceiling. Airport bus, trains and subway just outside the door. AE, DC, MC, V.

Sergel Plaza. Brunkebergstorg 91 (22 66 00). 407 rooms, very central. Features trees and waterfalls in the glass-roofed lobby. It has a restaurant, the *Café des Artistes*, saunas, solarium, bubblepool. AE, DC, MC, V.

Sheraton-Stockholm. Tegelbacken 6 (14 26 00). 476 rooms. Next to the railway station with a view of the Old Town and the Town Hall. The restaurant, *Le Bistro*, is open until 2.30 A.M. Piano bar, boutiques, garage. AE, DC, MC, V.

SAS Strand. Nybrokajen 9 (22 29 00). 134 rooms. Central location opposite the *Royal Dramatic Theater*. The building dates from 1912 and was completely renovated in 1984. Winter garden with a ceiling seven stories high and an outstanding gourmet restaurant. SAS airline check-in desk. AE, DC, MC, V.

Expensive

Continental. Vasagatan (24 40 20). 250 rooms. Opposite the railway station (RESO). Special low rates available in summer. *Nike* restaurant, *Bistro Chez Charles, Cafeteria Concorde.* AE, DC, MC, V.

Diplomat. Strandvägen 7C (63 58 00). 132 rooms. On the waterfront, within walking distance of Djurgården Park and Skansen as well as the city center. Turn-of-the-century atmosphere. Popular tea-house. AE, DC, MC, V.

Lady Hamilton. Storkyrkobrinken 5 (23 46 80). 35 rooms. A gem of a hotel. Built in 1470 and converted to an hotel in 1980. A large collection of antiques including one of George Romney's portraits of Lady Hamilton. The Storkyrkan (the cathedral) and the Royal Palace are neighbors. Cafeteria. AE, DC, MC, V.

Lord Nelson. Västerlånggatan 22 (23 23 90). 31 small rooms. Small hotel right in the middle of the Old Town and twinned, naturally enough, with the nearby Lady Hamilton. Atmosphere throughout is decidedly nautical, even down to the cabin-sized rooms. However, standards of comfort and service are high. Sauna; no restaurant. Cafeteria. AE, DC, MC, V.

Park Hotel. Karlavägen 43 (22 96 20). 206 rooms. Quiet, central location next to Humlegården Park, within walking distance of the city center. Restaurant, garden cafe, garage. (RESO). AE, DC, MC, V.

Reisen. Skeppsbron 12–14 (22 32 60). 125 rooms. A SARA hotel built behind the facade of three 17th-century houses. Has the *Quarter Deck* restaurant and the best piano bar in town. Saunas, pool, garage. AE, DC, MC, V.

SAS Arlandia. At Arlanda Airport (0760–618 00). 295 rooms. Five minutes by bus from the airport. Restaurant, bar, nightclub, cinema, sauna, indoor pool, tennis. Close to golf and bathing. AE, DC, MC, V.

Terminus. Vasagatan 20 (22 26 40). 155 rooms. Handy down-town location, if possibly noisy, opposite Central Station and close to airport buses. Popular restaurant, *Kasper*. AE, MC.

Moderate

Adlon. Vasagatan 42 (24 54 00). 58 rooms, 38 with bath. Central. AE, MC, V.

Alexandra. Magnus Ladulåsgatan 42 (84 03 20). 90 rooms. In the heart of Södermalm (south of Slussen). Five minutes to the city by the nearby subway. No restaurant. AE, DC, MC, V.

August Strindberg. Tegnérgatan 38 (32 50 06). 19 rooms in a building dating from 1890. Near a park, quiet, central. No elevator. AE, MC, V.

Birger Jarl. Tulegatan 8 (15 10 20). 252 rooms. Unlicensed. Quiet location within walking distance of Stureplan and the city center. Connected with neighboring church; has weekly services in English. Keep-fit area with a sauna and pool. Cafeteria. AE, DC, MC, V.

Bromma. Brommaplan (25 29 20). 141 rooms. Ten minutes by subway downtown, ten minutes by bus to Drottningholm Palace. Direct bus to Arlanda Airport. Restaurant, garage, small garden (RESO). AE, MC, V.

City. Slöjdgatan 7 (22 22 40). 302 rooms. Central. Close to the Hötorget market. Many smoke-free rooms; seven rooms specially equipped for the handicapped. Run by the Salvation Army. Unlicensed. Elegant restaurant. Magnificent indoor wintergarden. AE, DC, MC, V.

Eden. Sturegatan 10 (22 31 60). 55 rooms, some with balconies. On two top floors of an office building. Breakfast room with a summer terrace overlooking Humlegården Park. Central. AE, DC, MC, V.

Esplanade. Strandvägen 7A (63 07 40). 33 rooms. Within walking distance of Djurgården, Skansen and the city center. A turn-of-the-century atmosphere. Breakfast only. Closed in July. AE, DC, MC, V.

Flamingo. Hotellgatan 11, Solna (83 08 00). 130 rooms. Ten minutes by subway from the city. Restaurant, dancing, grillroom. Solna has a large shopping center. AE, DC, MC, V.

Flyghotellet. Brommaplan (26 26 20). 68 rooms. By subway, ten minutes from the city; by bus, ten minutes to Drottningholm Palace. Direct airport bus. AE, DC, MC, V.

Gamla Stan. Lilla Nygatan 25 (24 44 50). 59 rooms, 26 with baths. In the Old Town. Run by the Salvation Army. Cafeteria. No alcohol. AE, MC, V.

Karelia. Birger Jarlsgatan 35 (24 76 60). 103 rooms. A few minutes' walk from Stureplan. Finnish sauna and pool. Restaurant with Finnish and Russian specialties, dancing, nightclub. A bit of Finland in the heart of Stockholm. AE, DC, MC, V.

Mornington. Nybrogatan 53 (63 12 40). 137 rooms. Near the indoor market at Östermalmstorg, within walking distance of theaters and shopping. Elegant fish restaurant. AE, DC, MC, V.

Palace. St. Eriksgatan 115 (24 12 20). 214 rooms. Near the Haga Air Terminal. Sauna, garage. (RESO). AE, DC, MC, V.

Scandic Hotel. Järva Krog, Uppsalavägen, Solna (85 03 60). 215 rooms, of which 79 are smoke-free. North of the city on E 4. The airport bus stops here on request, and there's a regular bus service to the city. The *Rotisserie Musketör* on the 11th floor has a fine view of Brunnsviken Lake. AE, DC, MC, V.

Stockholm. Norrmalmstorg 1 (22 13 20). 91 rooms, 87 with baths. The hotel is on the top floor of an office building with Kungsträdgården Park and the *N.K.* department store just around the corner. Breakfast only. AE, MC, V.

Inexpensive

Anno 1647. Mariagränd 3 (44 04 80). 43 rooms, 12 with baths. Also some higher priced and elegant rooms. Located in a centuries-old building close to Slussen. Historic surroundings. A few steps from the subway and the ferry to Skansen. Breakfast only. No restaurant. AE, DC, MC, V.

Domus. Körsbärsvägen 1 (16 01 95). 78 rooms. Near subway. Family apartments with pantry available. Restaurant. AE, DC, MC, V.

Jerum. Studentbacken 21 (15 50 90 and June through Aug. 63 53 80). 120 rooms, all with showers. This student hostel is only open June 1 to Aug. 3. Close to Gärdet subway station, five minutes to the city. Cafeteria. AE, DC, MC, V.

Kom. Döbelnsgatan 17 (23 56 30). 87 rooms. Central, quiet. Kitchenette with refrigerator in all rooms. Sauna. Breakfast only. Near the subway. AE, DC, MC, V.

Kristineberg. Hjalmar Söderbergsväg 10 (13 03 00). 143 rooms, none with baths. Near a subway station, seven minutes from the city. Free sauna. Popular restaurant suitable for motorists. AE, DC, MC, V.

Zinken. Pipmakargränd 2 (58 50 11). 28 rooms. The hotel consists of a number of pavilions near Zinkensdam subway station. Large garden with play area, access to washing machine and kitchen. Also youth hostel. Sauna. No credit cards.

Camping

Ängby Camping. (A3) Bromma (37 04 20). West of Stockholm at Södra Ängby. A 2-star camping site. Beach at Lake Mälar. Rates approximately SEK 50 per night. Summer only.

Bredäng Camping. (A4) Skärholmen (97 70 71). A 3-star camping site at Ålgrytevägen in Sätra, ten km. (six miles) south of Stockholm. Follow the signs from E4. 500 meters (about 500 yards) to the subway, bathing, canoe rentals and so on. Rates approximately SEK 65 per night. Open all year.

Youth Hostels

af Chapman. Skeppsholmen (10 37 15). 136 beds. A 100-year-old sailing ship with the same view as the Grand Hotel in the historic heart of the city. Open Mar. to Dec. Stay limited to five nights.

Columbus Hotel. Tjärhövsgatan 11 (44 17 17). 120 beds. Open all year.

Gustaf af Klint. A ship at berth 153, at Stadsgården quay near Slussen (40 40 77). 51 beds. Open all night and all year.

Mälaren River Boat. Söder Mälarstrand 6 (44 43 85). 28 beds. Old ship converted into a privately run hostel. Near Slussen subway station.

Skeppsholmen Hostel. Västra Brobänken (20 25 06). Behind af Chapman. 132 beds. Open all year except Christmas/New Year period.

Zinken. Pipmakargränd 2 (68 57 86). 268 beds. Near Zinkensdamm subway station. Open all year.

There are also hostels at Gällnö, Möja, Arholma and Fjärdlång—all in the archipelago.

HOW TO GET AROUND. By subway and bus. The transport system is divided into zones. Tickets may be bought as coupons from ticket counters or from drivers. The basic fare is SEK 7 for journeys within one zone. Your ticket entitles you to unlimited transfers within one hour of the time your ticket was punched. Senior citizens and young people under 18 can travel for half fare.

A discount card with 18 coupons is available at SEK 45. However, if you plan to use the transportation system frequently, it's a good idea to buy a monthly card at SEK 150—you'll need a photo for this one. A one-day tourist card giving unlimited travel costs SEK 21 and a card for three days SEK 72. Children under 18 and senior citizens pay half-price. Two children up to 7 years travel free. Discount tickets and tourist cards are sold at *Pressbyrån* kiosks at the stations.

The Key to Stockholm card *("Stockholmskortet")* provides unlimited free transport on subway trains, suburban railway services and local buses through-out Greater Stockholm (except on airport bus services) and also offers free admission to 50 museums in the city plus free sightseeing trips by boat or bus and free parking on meters throughout the city. Cards valid for durations up to four days can be purchased at prices ranging from about SEK 70 to 225. It can be bought at a number of outlets, including the Tourist Center at Sweden House and the "Hotellcentralen" accommodation bureau at the central railway station.

By taxi. For a taxi ring 15 00 00 (15 04 00 for advance bookings). English-speaking drivers are available on request if you want to go sightseeing by taxi. You can also hail a taxi on the street—the sign *Ledig* indicates that the cab is for hire. They are not so readily available as, for example, in London, but the telephone booking service is very efficient, although the meter starts clocking up the kronor as soon as it sets off to pick you up. Taxis are fairly expensive in Stockholm, and more so at night. Tip about 10–15%.

TOURS. A number of sightseeing tours around Stockholm are available, and the boat trips are particularly good value. A two-hour "Under the Bridges of Stockholm" trip which takes you into the fresh water of Lake Mälaren and back into the salt water of the Baltic gives you a vivid impression of the maritime influence which has dominated the city's history. Numerous boat trips take you further out into the archipelago, most leaving from the quay outside the Grand Hotel, normally at 8 A.M. Meals are often available on these trips. There is an information kiosk outside the Grand and details are also available from the tourist office. In addition, there are walking tours around the Old Town every evening from the end of May to mid-September. Authorized city guides may also be hired through the tourist office; call 789 20 00, but book well in advance.

For excursions, further afield, try Sandhamn, a yachting center reached by boat from Stavsnäs, where races are held during July and August. A one-hour boat trip from Strömkajen in Stockholm will take you to Vaxholm, where an ancient fortress which is now a military museum guards the channel into Stockholm. A trip by boat or bus to the Gustavsberg porcelain factory might be worthwhile for reduced-price bargains. The porcelain museum is open weekdays only. A fascinating trip on Lake Mälar can be made on the classic steamer S/S *Mariefred* (daily; approximately SEK 110). Also of interest is the university town of Uppsala, 45 minutes north of Stockholm by train. The cathedral here is the seat of the Archbishop of Sweden. Some tours combine Uppsala with a visit to Sigtuna, Sweden's oldest town, with its 11th-century fortified church ruin and other monuments of Swedish history.

 MUSEUMS. The visitor to Stockholm has a wide choice of museums to see. The entrance fee is from SEK 5 to SEK 10, with children at half price or less but admission is free at most museums to holders of the Key to Stockholm card. Many museums are closed on Monday; they also tend to close earlier on Saturday and Sunday.

Armemuseum (Royal Army Museum). Located behind the Royal Dramatic Theater at Riddargatan 13. Exhibits from crossbows to automatic rifles and missiles. Equipment of the Swedish Army from many centuries. Open daily 11–4.

Biologiska Museet (Biological Museum). Next to Skansen. An old museum showing Nordic animals against panoramic natural backgrounds. Open daily 10–4. Open May through Sept. 10–5 daily; Mar. through Apr. and Oct. through Dec. 11–3 daily.

Etnografiska Museet (Ethnographical Museum). Djurgårdsbrunnsvägen 34. Famous collections from Third-World cultures. A newly-built museum. Bus 69. Open Mon. to Fri. 11–4, Sat. and Sun. 12–4; closed Mon.

Hallwyl Museum. Hamngatan 4, near Norrmalmstorg (10 21 66). A palatial building dating from around 1900. Fine collections of painting, sculpture, furniture, ceramics, arms etc. Guided tours only, in English at 1.15 P.M. daily June 12 to Aug. 31, except Sat. Closed Mon.

Historiska Museet (Museum of National Antiquities). Narvavägen 13–17. Treasures of the Vikings and their ancestors. In same building as the **Royal Cabinet of Coin**, which includes the world's largest coin. Bus 44 and 47. Open daily 11–4; closed Mon.

Leksaksmuseum (Toy Museum). Mariatorget 1C. Thousands of toys, dolls, dolls houses, tin soldiers etc. on four floors. Two large model railways are usually demonstrated on weekends. Subway Mariatorget. Open Tues. to Fri. 10–4, Sat. and Sun. 12–4; closed Mon.

Liljevalchs Konsthall (Liljevalch Art Gallery). Djurgårdsvägen 60. Temporary exhibitions, mostly of Swedish contemporary art. Café Blå Porten. Bus 47. Open Tues. and Thurs. 11–9, Wed., Fri., Sat. and Sun. 11–5.

Livrustkammaren (Royal Armory). In the cellars of the Royal Palace with entrance at Slottsbacken. Swedish State collections of historical objects, such as costumes, arms and armory of Swedish royalty from 16th century on. Open Mon. to Fri. 10–4, Sat. and Sun. 11–4. Closed Mon., Sept. to Apr.

Medelhavsmuseet (Mediterranean Museum). Fredsgatan 2 at Gustav Adolfs Torg. 2,500 year-old terracotta sculptures of Cypriot warriors. Also a large Egyptian collection and an exhibition from the Islamic countries. Open Tues. 11–9, Wed. to Sun. 11–4; closed Mon.

Millesgården. Lidingö. Former residence of Swedish-American sculptor Carl Milles. He had his home at Lidingö in later years, where he collected not only some of his own work, but also other outstanding pieces from several eras. He died here in 1955 at the age of 80, still at work. Sparkling fountains and monuments with a view of Stockholm as a background. (The Orpheus Fountain outside the Concert House was made by Milles in 1936). Subway to Ropsten and then by bus. Open May through Sept. 10–5 daily; Mar. through Apr., and Oct. through Dec., 11–3 daily.

Moderna Museet (Museum of Modern Art and Photography). On Skeppsholmen, behind the sailing ship youth hostel *af Chapman.* Paintings by Scandinavian artists and Picasso, Dali, Matisse, Warhol and many more. Open Tues. to Fri. 11–9, Sat. and Sun. 11–5; closed Mon.

Nationalmuseet (National Art Museum). A few steps from the Grand Hotel. Great masters from 1500 to 1900. Also prints, drawings and applied art from the Renaissance to the present day. Cafeteria and good shop. Concerts every Tues. in July and Aug. Open Tues. 10–9, (10–5 July and Aug.), Wed. to Sun. 10–4; closed Mon.

Nordiska Museet (Nordic Museum). Djurgården. Largest collection of objects showing the progress of civilization in Sweden since 1500. Magnificent specimens of rural art. Lovely collection of bridal crowns and much more. Bus 47. Open Mon. to Wed. 10–4, Thurs. 10–8, Fri. 10–4, Sat. and Sun. 12–5; closed Fri. Sept. to May.

Sjöhistoriska Museet (National Maritime Museum). Djurgårdsbrunnsvägen 24. Collections illustrating history of Swedish navy and merchant marine. Unique ship models. Bus 69. Open daily 10–5.

Stockholms Stadsmuseum (City Museum). At Slussen subway station. The history of Stockholm, illustrated by many archeological finds. Models of the former palaces "Tre Kronor" (Three Crowns) and "Non Pareil." Pleasant cafeteria. Open Tues. to Thurs. 11–7, Fri. to Mon. 11–5.

Strindbergmuseet. Blå Tornet, Drottninggatan 85. Home of author August Strindberg. Open Tues. to Sat. 10–4, Sun. 12–5.

Tekniska Museet (Science and Technology Museum). Museivägen, on the way to the Kaknäs Tower. Models of machines illustrating developments in technical engineering and industry. Vintage aeroplanes, cars' engines; computers, telecommunications. A mine with shafts etc. Cafeteria. Bus 69 from Karlaplan. Open Mon. to Fri. 10–4, Sat. and Sun. 12–4.

Thielska Galleriet (Thiel Art Gallery). Djurgården near Blockhusudden. Private collection of Scandinavian and French art from around 1900. Beautiful surroundings. Bus 69 from Karlaplan. Open daily 12–4 (from 1 on Sun.).

Waldemarsudde. Djurgården. Former home of Prince Eugen, a great-grand uncle to the present King. He was a well-known painter and many of the Prince's own works are displayed here. Also Nordic collections. The turn-of-the-century house is surrounded by a beautiful garden on the shores of the Baltic. Cafeteria. Bus 47. Open Tues. to Sun. 11–5; Mon. 7–9. Winter opening 11–4, closed Mon. and most of Dec.

Wasavarvet (Wasa Museum). On Djurgården, on the way to Skansen just below the Liljevalchs Konsthall. The salvaged 17th-century man-of-war, *Wasa.* She sank in Stockholm harbor on her maiden voyage in 1628. Rediscovered in 1956, she was raised and drydocked in 1961 and has been painstakingly restored. This is the oldest preserved warship in the world. A film of the *Wasa* rebirth is shown every hour. Guided tours in English. Cafeteria, souvenir shop. Bus 47. Open daily 10–5 (June 8 to Aug. 17, 9.30–7).

 PARKS, ZOOS AND GARDENS. Djurgården (Royal Deer Park) and Skansen. A beautiful island covered in pathways, meadows and trees. Also a marina, many museums, Gröna Lund amusement park, Skansen and its zoo, aquarium, open air theater and various displays, and much more. Rent a bike near the bridge or take a leisurely stroll. You can also rent canoes. In summer most of the roads are closed to cars. Bus 47 or ferry from Slussen or Nybroplan (summer only).

Fjällgatan. To get a good view of the Old Town and the harbor, take the subway to Slussen and walk up on Katarina Bangatan to Fjällgatan. Most sight-seeing buses stop here for a short time.

Kungsträdgården (King's Garden). Easy to find, just across the rushing water from the Royal Palace. It contains the striking statue of King Charles XII (Karl den Tolfte) with his arm raised pointing east. On the right is the Royal Opera House, and behind that the elm trees, once threatened to make way for a new subway station, but saved by city-wide protests in 1971. The station was built elsewhere. Have a sandwich under the elms at the teahouse. The fountain in the park, built in 1873, features pictures of Nordic mythology. There are many activities in the park in summer. You can listen to music, learn to dance the Swedish *Hambo* or play chess; in winter you can skate. A meeting place for tourists and others.

Långholmsparken. Below Västerbron on the south side. Take the path to the top for the view. Some former prison buildings are still here—debate continues over the possibility of using them for a youth hostel or hotel. The little cottage is open for coffee when the flag is up. Subway Hornstull.

Skinnarviksparken. Beautiful panorama from this park. Nearest subway is Zinkensdamm. Walk towards the lake and up the mountain past some newly restored historic buildings.

HISTORIC BUILDINGS AND SITES. Drottningholm Palace. On an island in Lake Mälar, a few kilometers from Stockholm. Reminiscent of Versailles, a magnificent 17th-century French-style building. Also in the grounds are the lovely Chinese Palace and the original court theater, with its 18th-century settings and stage machinery in perfect working order. Theater museum. Subway to Brommaplan and bus or boat from Stadshusbron. The Palace, Court Theater and Chinese Palace are open daily May through Aug. 11–4.30, and 1–3.30 during Sept.

Gamla Stan (Old Town). Follow a lane called Storkyrkobrinken from the Great Church, past buildings that are centuries old, to a square at the base of the hill called Riddarhustorget. The two dominating buildings in the square, Riddarhuset (House of Nobility) and the white palace to its right, both date from the 17th century. The latter now houses the Supreme Court.

Haga Palace and Haga Pavilion. On the city limits of Stockholm, in Haga Park near Brunnsviken. Former home of the late Crown Prince Gustav Adolf. The Pavilion is the more interesting building—a miniature summer palace built by Gustav III in the late-18th century. Bus 52 to Haga Air Terminal. Guided tours every hour. Open May through Aug., Tues. to Sun. 12–3; Sept., Tues. to Sun. 1–3.

Kaknästornet (Kaknäs Tower). Djurgården. T.V. tower, 155 meters (508 ft.) high. Indoor and outdoor platforms with breathtaking view. Cafeteria and restaurant, tourist bureau and souvenir shop. Bus 69. Open Oct. through Mar., daily 9–6; Apr. and Sept., daily 9 A.M.–10 P.M.; May to Aug., daily 9–12 midnight.

Kungliga Slottet (Royal Palace). Completed 1760. Hall of State (contains the King's silver throne), the Chapel Royal (Sunday service open to the public), the Apartments of State and of King Oscar and Queen Sophie, as well as the Guest Apartments are all open to the public daily. Also the Palace Museum (classical sculptures and antiquities), the Royal Treasury, with its collection of Crown Jewels, and the Royal Armory. All or part of the palace may be closed when state visits, royal dinners etc. are held. Changing of the guard, June through Aug., Mon. to Fri. at 12.10 P.M., Sun. at 1.10 P.M. Jan. through May, Wed., Sat. and Sun.; Sept. through Dec., Wed. and Sun. There is no band playing in the winter.

Mårten Trotzigs Gränd (Yard-wide Lane). In the Old Town, at the end of Prästgatan, leading down to Västerlånggatan. One of the narrowest thoroughfares in the world, scarcely a yard (a meter) wide.

Riddarholm Church. On Riddarholm Island. This is the Swedish Pantheon; burial place of 17 Swedish kings over about four centuries. Subway Gamla Stan. Open May through Aug., daily 10–3, Sun. 1–3.

Stadshuset (Town Hall). Completed 1923, it is the symbol of Stockholm and of considerable architectural interest. The tower, with a magnificent view, is open May through Sept., daily 10–3. Guided tours of the Town Hall, Mon. to Sat. at 10 A.M.; Sat., Sun. and holidays at 10 A.M. and 12 noon.

Storkyrkan (Great Church). Across the street from the south side of the Royal Palace. Believed to be the oldest building in the city, dating from about 1250. Contains Ehrenstal's *Last Judgement,* one of the world's largest paintings, and other art treasures. As Stockholm's cathedral, this is a living church with a congregation and sightseeing during services is not allowed. Occasionally there are sound and light performances.

Swedish Academy. North side of Stortorget, near the Royal Palace. Historic building, the headquarters of the Swedish Academy, which awards the Nobel Prize in literature.

SPORTS. Tennis. There are a number of indoor tennis courts as well as outdoor courts at: Hjorthagen, in Jäg-mästaregatan; Smedslätten, in Gustav Adolfs Park; South Ångby, in Färjestadsvägen; Enskede, Mälarhöjd-en, and Älvsiö sports grounds.

Golf. Golfing enthusiasts have a choice of 14 18-hole courses. Among the best are: Stockholm Golf Club, Kevinge, train from Östra Station or underground to Mörby Centrum; Djursholms Golf Club, Eddavägen Station, train from Östra Station; Drottningholm Golf Club, bus from St. Eriksgatan; Lidingö Golf Club, Sticklinge, underground to Ropsten thence bus; Saltsjöbaden Golf Club, Tattby Station, train from Saltsjöbanan Station, Slussen (change at Igelboda); on Värmdö, at Hemmestavik (bus from Slussen).

Swimming. Långholmsparken or Mariebergsbadet. It's quite something to be able to swim in the center of a big city these days.

Fishing. You may fish free of charge from the bridges of Stockholm; the water is cleaner today than 50 years ago and salmon have been caught just in front of the Royal Palace. *Fritidsfiskarna* (19 78 20) can arrange to rent you tackle, if you give them a few days' notice.

Winter sports. There are a number of ski trails in the vicinity of Stockholm and in the Södertörn and Roslagen areas. The track at Nacka is floodlit for night skiing. Both Fiskartorpet and Hammarby have slalom runs, lifts and ski jumps. For ice skating, there are the Stadium, Östermalm Sports Ground, Tennis Stadium and Johanneshov Rink at Sandstuyägen; many parks, including central Kungsträdgården, have winter rinks.

You can rent downhill skiing equipment and cross-country skis at Skid och Brä-doktorn, Sturegatan 20 (63 75 75).

Spectator sports. If you want to be a spectator, call 22 18 40 and Miss Frida will tell you about the sporting events of the day in a tape recorded message.

Biking and canoeing. Bikes and canoes are available for rent at Djurgården bridge.

MUSIC, MOVIES AND THEATERS. Music. Stock-holm's two musical centers are the *Royal Opera House* and the *Stockholm Concert House.* The Royal Opera, located just across the bridge from the Royal Palace, has a season running from mid-August until about June 10. The Ballet Festival is in the first week of June.

The concert season lasts from about the middle of September to about the middle of May. The Stockholm Concert Association Orchestra is in regular service at the Concert House and is fully up to international standards. But of even greater interest perhaps is the veritable parade of top international virtuosos and guest conductors, representing the cream of European, British and American talent.

Every day during the summer, concerts and other kinds of entertainment are held in the open air at *Skansen.* Also, the *Gröna Lund* amusement park, open mid-April to mid-September, has daily open-air performances with Swedish and foreign artists. Between June 15 and the end of August, there are free concerts in the city's many parks. In the *Kungsträdgården* there are daily recorded concerts and, three evenings a week at least, free entertainment on the outdoor stage, often featuring leading variety artists.

A unique experience is to attend a concert at the *National Museum* (Art Gallery), held four times during August. Occasionally there are also concerts in the *Royal Palace.*

For information about concerts and theaters (including English-speaking theaters), call at the kiosk on Norrmalmstorg where you can also buy reduced price tickets for same-day performances.

Movies. English and American movies dominate. They are shown with Swedish sub-titles and are often released at the same time as they appear in London or New York. See the evening papers for programs. The advertisements usually mention the English as well as the Swedish title.

Theaters. Several theaters specialize in light opera—playing classics and modern musicals. It's great fun hearing and seeing a familiar perennial in a strange theater and a strange language (though many may find the language barrier insuperable). Season: Sept. to mid-June.

The *Royal Dramatic Theater*—scene of the debuts of Greta Garbo and Ingrid Bergman—actually consists of two theaters, one for major performances and a smaller one for those of more limited public interest. A number of the plays presented here and at other Stockholm theaters are hits still running in New York or London. Season: Sept. through May.

Particularly recommended is the *Court Theater* of Drottningholm Palace, a few minutes to a half-hour from downtown Stockholm by car or bus (or 50 minutes by boat). This is an 18th-century theater which was somehow lost sight of, closed up for years, and when reopened a few decades ago was found to be in its original condition. The repertoire consists almost entirely of operas and ballets contemporary with the theater: in other words, of works written for that kind of stage. Seeing a performance there is a unique theater event. Performances during May, June, July, August and September, two to four evenings a week. Again, call at the kiosk on Norrmalmstorg for information and tickets.

 SHOPPING. Shopping in Stockholm tends to be expensive, but you can be sure of the quality. You can also take advantage of the Scandinavian Taxfree scheme, under which a part of your sales tax will be refunded at the airport. Ask for details at the shop; you need special receipts to present at the airport, harbor or on board ship. See also "Shopping" in *Facts at Your Fingertips.* When you see the word REA, it means there's a sale in progress. The best REAs are after Christmas and mid-summer.

First shopping stop in Stockholm should be the *Nordiska Kompaniet,* known as N.K., at Hamngatan 18–20. This store is a sort of combination Neiman-Marcus and Harrods, with a few specialties of its own thrown in; you can find almost anything you might want to buy here. Opposite the N.K. is the *Gallerian shopping arcade,* where you can find shoes, clothing, books, antiques, perfume, cameras and much more. On the other side of the fountain is *Åhléns,* a huge department store near Sergels Torg, Drottninggatan and Hötorget. And here also is the *P.U.B.* department store, in buildings on both sides of Drottninggatan with a tunnel connection. The P.U.B. also has an extensive range, but is less luxurious and lower-priced. It faces on to Hötorget and the Concert Hall, in an area where shops of all kinds can be found.

In Gamla Stan many specialty shops can be found on Västerlånggatan. If you walk towards Slussen and to the right on Hornsgatan, you come to a hill called Puckeln, where many small and interesting art galleries are to be found. Handicrafts are on sale at *Svensk Hemslöjd,* Sveavägen 44, the *Stockholm Handicraft Shop* at Drottninggatan 18, *De Fyras Bod* at Birger Jarlsgatan 12, and at *Handarbetets Vänner* (Friends of Needlework) at Djurgårdsslätten 82.

There are shopping malls in suburbs such as Vällingby, Kista and Skärholmen, where you can also find the huge furniture store *IKEA,* and an indoor flea market which is open on Saturdays and Sundays. *Casselryds,* at Skärholmen, is one of the largest stockists of Swedish crystal.

 RESTAURANTS. Since restaurants play such an important part in Stockholm life, a fairly extensive list is given here. Most have liquor licenses, though do remember that alcohol is very expensive. Some of the downtown establishments close for three or four weeks during the summer. As in all big cities, there are many types of restaurant in Stockholm, such as Greek, Japanese, Chinese, Korean. All the main hotels have their own restaurants. If you are on a budget, look for bargains such as Sunday Specials, happy hours, all-in menus etc. You'll find details in the newspapers next to the entertainments section.

Expensive

Aurora. Munkbron 11 (21 93 59). Located in a beautiful 300-year-old house in the Old Town with pleasant small rooms in vaults. Charcoal grill. Excellent food and service. AE, DC, MC, V.

Clas på Hörnet. Surbrunnsgatan 20 (16 51 30). One of the most unusual settings in Stockholm—on the ground floor of an elegant restored 200-year-old town house which is also an exclusive hotel. Excellent international and Swedish cuisine. AE, DC, MC, V.

Coq Blanc. Regeringsgatan 111 (11 61 53). Was once a theater; stage and stalls intact. Excellent food. Budget-priced lunch menu. AE, DC, MC, V.

Coq Roti. Sturegatan 19 (10 25 67). A gourmet restaurant run by professionals; French cuisine in sophisticated setting. AE, DC, MC, V.

Den Gyldene Freden. Österlånggatan 51 (10 12 59). Old Town. Medieval cellars with historical traditions and atmosphere. Lute singers some evenings. Oldest restaurant in Sweden. AE, DC, MC, V.

Eriks. On quay-berth 17, Strandvägskajen (60 60 60). This former sand barge has been converted into a de luxe restaurant. In summer enjoy the view from the deck. Choose your own fish. AE, DC, MC, V.

L'Escargot. Scheelegatan 8 (53 05 77). As the name implies, snails are a specialty of the house, but it is more popular for its daily six-course gastronomic menu. AE, DC, MC, V.

Fem Små Hus. Nygränd 10 (10 04 82). In the Old Town. Its name means "five small houses." Many small rooms in vaults. Excellent international cuisine and Swedish specialties. AE, DC, MC, V.

Garbo. Blekingegatan 32 (40 12 07). It was here that Greta Garbo was born in 1905 so the atmosphere is very movie oriented. AE, DC, MC, V.

Gourmet. Tegnérgatan 10 (31 43 98). Lives up to its name: one of the best French restaurants in town. Pleasant atmosphere. AE, DC, MC, V.

Grand Hotel. S. Blasieholmshamnen 8 (22 10 20). Excellent restaurant (terrace outside in the summer) with marvelous views of the Royal Palace and the Old Town. This is the place for *Smörgåsbord* in relaxed and sophisticated surroundings. AE, DC, MC, V.

K.B. or Konstnärshuset. Smålandsgatan 7, near Norrmalmstorg (11 02 32). Eat and drink in intimate surroundings in the heart of town. Murals by Swedish artists who paid for their drinks with paintings. AE, DC, MC, V.

Latona. Västerlånggatan 79 (11 32 60). Cavernous cellar-restaurant in the heart of the Old Town, by Järntorget. Scores for atmosphere, service and excellent food. AE, DC, MC, V.

Mälardrottningen. Riddarholmen (24 36 00). Floating restaurant and hotel on Barbara Hutton's former private yacht. Seafood specialties. Reservation essential. AE, DC, MC, V.

Operakällaren. In the Opera House facing Kungsträdgården, the waterfront and the Royal Palace (11 11 25). World-famous for international cuisine and the atmosphere. AE, DC, MC, V.

Riche and Teatergrillen. Birger Jarlsgatan 4 (10 70 22). The *Riche* side has a veranda on the street. Fine paintings create an elegant ambience. Roast beef—not perhaps one of the most obvious things to expect in Stockholm—is served from a silver trolley every day. The *Teatergrillen,* or *Theater Grill* (tel. 10 70 44) is more intimate and lives up to its name in attracting some of the theater crowd. Good for a quiet dinner. The grill is closed in July. AE, DC, MC, V.

Solliden. Skansen (60 10 55). On the heights at Stockholm's favorite pleasure grounds, ten minutes from the center of town. Open May to Aug. Wonderful view of the city and harbor. Also self-service on the ground floor and a big outdoor restaurant in summer. AE, DC, MC, V.

Stallmästargården. Norrtull, near the Haga Air Terminal (24 39 10). Historic inn with view of Brunnsviken Lake. Coffee in the courtyard, with a lovely garden, after a good meal on a summer evening is a delightful experience. AE, DC, MC, V.

Stortorgskällaren. Stortorget 7 (10 55 33). Charming medieval cellar in the Old Town near the Cathedral and the Royal Palace. Adjoining a fish restaurant with the same management. AE, DC, MC, V.

Ulriksdals Wärdshus. In a fine park near Ulriksdal Palace (85 08 15). 15 minutes by car or bus 540 from Humlegården Park. Old Swedish inn with famed *Smörgåsbord.* AE, DC, MC, V.

Moderate

Bäckahästen. Hamngatan 2 (20 01 36). Modern décor; openair service on pavement in summer. Good food and large portions. Closed Mon. AE, DC, MC, V.

Birger Bar. Birger Jarlsgatan 5 (20 72 10). Popular restaurant specializing in Italian cuisine. AE, DC, MC, V.

Cattelin. Storkyrkobrinken 9, in Old Town (20 18 18). Seafood a specialty, but there's also a bistro. Members of Parliament meet here. AE, DC, MC, V.

Colibri. Corner Drottninggatan and Adolf Fredriks Kyrkogatan (10 81 20). Plank steak.

Daily News Café. Kungsträdgården in Sverigehuset (21 56 55). Good food. Swedish and foreign newspapers to hand (but not on the menu). AE, DC, MC, V.

Gondolen. (40 22 22). Suspended under the gangway of the Katarina elevator at Slussen. View of the harbor and the Old Town. AE, DC, MC, V.

La Grenouille. Grev Turegatan 16 (20 10 00). French-style establishment with three separate restaurants in different price brackets. AE, DC, MC, V.

N.K. Department Store. Opposite Sverigehuset. A shoppers' favorite, with a restaurant, salad bar and coffee shop. AE, DC, MC, V.

Östergök. Kommendörsgatan 46 (61 15 07). Specializes in fish, but there's also a steakhouse and a pizzeria here. Popular. AE, DC, MC, V.

Rodolfino. Stora Nygatan 1 (11 84 97). Italian specialties, though not exclusively, in small, chic spot in the Old Town, by the Riddarhuset. Popular with the younger crowd; good food and service. AE, DC, MC, V.

Stadshuskällaren. Stadshuset (City Hall), (50 54 54). Rustic atmosphere in the cellar of the City Hall overlooking Lake Mälaren. AE, DC, MC, V.

Sturehof. Stureplan 2 (14 27 50). A fairly large, unpretentious restaurant, which makes fish its business. Pub in old English style. Quieter in the back of the restaurant. Just in the middle of town. AE, DC, MC, V.

Vau-de-Ville. Hamngatan 17 (21 25 22). French-bistro atmosphere. Excellent food at reasonable prices. Chosen as Stockholm's 1986 "Restaurant of the Year." AE, DC, MC, V.

Inexpensive

Gröna Linjen. Mäster Samuelsgatan 10, third floor (11 27 90). Good for lunch. Vegetarian. No credit cards.

Tehuset (the tea house). Under the elms in Kungsträdgården Park. Lively and chic outdoor place. Have a hot sandwich there at noon and watch the Royal Guard march by. Summer only. No credit cards.

Zum Franziskaner. Skeppsbron 44 (11 83 30). German-style restaurant on the waterfront in the Old Town. Food is reasonable and service very friendly. Popular. AE, MC, V.

In the **Gallerian shopping arcade** there are several good places to eat, including *Glada Laxen* (M), a café specializing in fish, but often with lines waiting at lunchtime. Also the *Pizzeria* (I), with a salad table and other dishes besides pizza. On the balcony, you can find *Edelweiss,* with a choice of salads and cakes.

The indoor market at *Östermalmshallen* has many food shops. At this 100-year-old indoor market visit *Gerdas* fish shop, where you can get an excellent lunch at a reasonable price in unusual and noisy surroundings. In the same building, on the second floor, you can find the biggest salad table in town. It's called *Örtagården* (the Herb Garden) (I) (62 17 28).

Look out for the special lunch offers available at almost all restaurants Mon. to Fri. 10–2. A main course plus drinks, salad, bread and butter costs about SEK 30–40.

NIGHTLIFE. Stockholm has a wide range of nightspots to choose from, the names and ownership of which change fairly frequently. See the last page in the daily papers for what's on and where. There are no real nightlife bargains and you should expect a supper in one of these nightspots to cost you between SEK 200 and 300. When there is a show it could cost you more. It's also a good idea to book in advance.

Entry to a pub with live music would be about SEK 25–45. Also many restaurants have dancing a few nights a week.

Aladdin. Barnhusgatan 12 (10 09 32). Oriental decor. Big dance floor.

Atlantic. Teatergatan 2 (21 89 07). Mixed, elegant crowd.

Bacchi Wapen. Järntorgsgatan 5 (11 66 71). As well as the restaurant, there's a disco, piano bar and café.

Börsen. Jakobsgatan 6 (10 16 00). Stockholm's biggest "show restaurant," with international artists.

Café Opera. Operakajen 9 (11 00 26). Very popular, so get there as early as possible.

Club Alexandra. Birger Jarlsgatan 29 (10 46 46). Most famous nightspot in town, located in Stockholm Plaza Hotel.

Cindy's Bar. Amaranten Hotel (54 10 60).

Daily News Café. Kungsträdgården (21 56 55). Central, near the N.K. department store. Restaurant, bar and disco.

Engelen. Kornhamnstorg 59 (10 07 22). In an old pharmacy in the Old Town. Long lines and mixed crowd, but more for the younger set.

Fasching. Kungsgatan 63 (21 93 65). Stockholm's biggest jazz club.

Gamlingen. Stora Gråmunkegränd (20 57 93). Again, for the younger set.

Kaos. Stora Nygatan 21 (20 58 80). In the Old Town. Wide range of music. Young, mixed crowd.

King Creole. Kungsgatan 18 (24 47 00). Some evenings features "old-time" dancing.

Stampen. Stora Gråmunkegränd (20 57 93). Old Town. A pub with "trad" jazz music.

Bars

There are piano bars at the Hotel Sheraton, Amaranten, Reisen, Continental, Sergel Plaza and Malmen.

If you want something to eat after midnight, there are a few places near Norrmalmstorg such as **Collage**, Smålandsgatan 2 (10 01 95), **Café La Clé**, Hamngatan 6 (20 87 00) and **Monte Carlo**, Sveavägen 23 (11 00 25).

STOCKHOLM ENVIRONS AND GOTLAND

The Capital as an Excursion Center

Stockholm is, in a literal sense, two-faced. It turns at one and the same time to two diametrically opposed worlds which have really only one thing in common—water. To the east the world is harsh, rough, rugged, primeval and its water is the treacherous salt water of the sea. To the west the world is friendly, civilized, the cradle of an ancient culture, and its water is the sweet water shed by farmland and forest. The former is the Stockholm Archipelago, the latter the valley of the sprawling, multi-armed Lake Mälar.

The Swedes have given the archipelago a name which is both romantic and descriptive, Skärgården, or Garden of Skerries. There are thousands of them, large and small, some wooded, some rocky, some even cultivated, separated by broad and narrow channels, indented by bays —in short, a unique seascape. The archipelago has supported a small and hardy farming and fishing population for centuries, living out quiet lives almost unnoticed until a few decades ago. Now the skerries are also a summer playground. And one of the great joys is convenience: you can get well out into the archipelago and back in a few hours.

56

Exploring the Stockholm Environs

Here are some of the principal summer resorts and sights, of which several are only an hour or so from Stockholm.

Sandhamn. Yachting center at the extreme eastern edge of the archipelago on the open Baltic Sea. Sandhamn's original importance was as a pilot station, but it is now also a popular summer resort because of its sandy beaches and good sailing facilities. The Royal Swedish Yacht Club has a clubhouse here and arranges a number of international races in the July-August regatta season. Daily boat connections from Stockholm. Special packages are available at an all-in price which includes the round trip to Sandhamn by boat as well as overnight accommodations with breakfast at the comfortable Sandhamns Hotel.

Vaxholm. Characterized by an ancient fortress guarding the channel into Stockholm. (The German Field-Marshal von Moltke is said to have laughed on only two occasions in his life—one of them was at the sight of Vaxholm Fortress.) The fortress is now open as a museum showing the military defense of Stockholm over the centuries. Vaxholm is a small but progressive town with good tennis courts and bathing.

Tyresö Castle. An ancient estate southeast of Stockholm, only 40 minutes from Ringvägen, (bus No. 10). The estate has belonged to some of Sweden's outstanding noble families since the Middle Ages. Its last owner willed it to the Nordiska Museum in 1930. Interesting art, including 18th-century French paintings.

Nynäshamn. A seaside town. Good beaches. Port of departure for steamers to the Baltic Sea island of Gotland.

Here is an important note: *Some parts of the archipelago are defense zones, closed to foreigners.* To avoid possible inconvenience, check before starting. If you put ashore at a strange point, look for the presence of a sign which might indicate that it is a prohibited area. They are posted in several languages, including English. If, for any reason, you wish to enter one of the zones—it may be quite possible that some Swedish friend or acquaintance of yours has a summer cottage within one—you can apply to the "Kustartilleri-stationen" in Vaxholm. The regulations are fairly strict, and there is no guarantee that such an application will always be approved.

Sigtuna, Skokloster and Gripsholm Castles

Sigtuna was founded about the year 1000 by Sweden's first Christian king, Olof Skötkonung, and for a time it was the chief political and religious center of the country. Sigtuna is located north of Stockholm, a little more than half way to Uppsala. It is not on the main railway line; you change to a bus in Märsta. A visit to Sigtuna can suitably be combined with an outing to Uppsala. During the summer there is an excursion by boat from the City Hall bridge in Stockholm to Sigtuna, with a free guided tour of the city, continuing to Uppsala and returning by train. There is also a twice-weekly excursion from Stockholm by bus taking in both Uppsala and Sigtuna.

The Sigtuna sun rose rapidly and sank rapidly. Bearing witness to its brief age of glory are the ruins of the first stone edifices erected in Sweden, pre-Norman churches dedicated to St. Per, St. Olof, and St. Lars. These were also fortresses, designed as much with an eye to defense as to the glorification of God. They overlooked a thriving community for nearly 200 years, during which the first Swedish coins were minted and Anglo-Saxon missionaries pushed the conversion of the Swedes.

Despite the stone churches, the city was more or less destroyed in 1187 by Vikings from across the Baltic, but lived on, thanks partly to the Dominican Monastery. The Reformation delivered a new blow, the monasteries were closed, and Sigtuna sank into obscurity. In modern times it has begun to flourish again as an educational and religious center.

You will find Sigtuna more idyllic than exciting. Note the charm of its narrow main street—Stora Gatan—which is said to follow its original route of 950 years ago and is known as the oldest street in Sweden. The layers of earth here have furnished the archeologists with a wealth of finds, from which they have reconstructed the life of various centuries. Maria Church, once the Dominican Monastery church was one of the first brick churches in the whole Lake Mälar valley, but only a few ruins remain of the monastery itself. St. Olof's Church gives you a good idea of the military aspects of early church architecture—it dates from about 1050. The construction material was rough granite blocks, the windows are mere loopholes, and the entrance just large enough to admit one person at a time.

On the heights overlooking the city you will find the modern institutions which have given new life to Sigtuna. One is the Sigtuna Foundation, sponsored by the Swedish Church, which includes a continuation college for adults, a chapel, and a guest house—the latter popular among authors as a good place to work. The others are the Sigtuna Academy and the Humanistic Academy, both boarding schools, and the College for Laymen, for instruction in volunteer parish work. Note also the unique little 18th-century Town Hall—supposed to be the smallest in the country—and a number of rune stones. About 16 kilometers (ten miles) northeast of Sigtuna lies Skokloster Castle.

Skokloster has recently been sold to the Swedish State. It has the richest collection of art treasures from the Swedish Imperial Era, and its display of weapons is outstanding.

The castle was built between 1654 and 1679 by Carl Gustaf Wrangel, one of Gustavus Adolphus' best-known field marshals. When he died it went to a relative, Count Nils Brahe, and was passed on from one Brahe to another until the family died out about 20 years ago. It then came into the hands of a related family, the von Essens. For the most part the furniture, paintings, and tapestries antedate the Thirty Years' War. The library contains some 30,000 volumes. A motor museum is the last private owner's contribution to his forefather's collection, and there is now a hotel and vacation center in the grounds.

A pleasant place for a short excursion from Stockholm is Sturehov, 22 kilometers (14 miles) west of the city. This is an old mansion and estate belonging to the city of Stockholm and used for civic entertainment, but it is also open to the public. The mansion is an exceptionally fine example of 18th-century Swedish architecture and interior design, and contains about a dozen porcelain stoves from the famous Marieberg factory, apart from many other treasures.

Gripsholm Castle is an ideal day-excursion by boat from Stockholm. You ride three pleasant hours through the beautiful scenery of Lake Mälar, stop in Gripsholm long enough for an inspection of the old castle and a good lunch, and get back to Stockholm by early evening. As a castle site, Gripsholm dates back to some time in the 1300s but the present towered structure was begun about 1535 on the orders of

King Gustav Vasa. Fully restored, livable and well maintained—after a period as a state prison—Gripsholm today is an outstanding museum, with a large and fine collection of historical portraits.

In the castle, note particularly the little theater. It, like Drottning-holm Theater, owes its existence to drama-loving King Gustav III, and has been preserved in its original condition. Although much smaller, in the opinion of many it is vastly more beautiful and full of atmosphere than its counterpart at Drottningholm. Nearby is the prison tower, where the tragic King Erik XIV (whom Strindberg made the central figure of one of his most powerful dramas) was held captive after his dethronement. The collection of portraits was begun by King Gustav Vasa himself in the 16th century, and now numbers nearly 3,000 paint-ings, with emphasis on Swedish royalty but with a number of royal figures from other lands.

In the courtyards note particularly the rune stones, among the best preserved to be found, and the artfully designed bronze cannons, war booty from the Swedish wars with Russia centuries ago. (Incidentally, the Soviet government has made unsuccessful efforts to get them re-turned to Russia. The Swedes, however, seem inclined to keep these memories of days when inferior Swedish forces often licked the tar out of the Czar's finest.)

Visby, City of Ruins and Roses

If you choose to visit Visby—the "City of Ruins and Roses" on the storied isle of Gotland in the Baltic Sea—during the off-season, say early November, you will find the short flight from Stockholm unfor-gettable. The sunset will provide one of those incredible displays of color that are to be found only in this part of the world.

At the Visby airport, you will be amazed to see a bed of red, red roses, in this northern corner of the world, still blooming. According to the inhabitants, roses are sometimes to be seen blooming in even December and January. Whatever the season, the red has a special brilliance resulting from the composition of the soil.

You feel something in the very atmosphere of Visby, a sense of the Middle Ages living on into the 20th century. Looping around the city is the magnificent wall, completely embracing it on all but the sea side. When you enter one of the 13th- or 14th-century gates, you find this special atmosphere among the beautiful buildings. Stepped, gabled houses date back to Visby's era of greatness. And everywhere are buildings centuries old, some of them well preserved, others, particular-ly the churches, in a gaunt state of disrepair that adds to their charm. Try, if you can, to see the view from the Powder Tower in the moon-light. This tower, serving as one of the main anchors of the wall, near the sea on the north side of town, is perhaps the oldest of the watch towers that rise up at intervals along the medieval wall.

The history of the island of Gotland, and the capital city Visby, goes back thousands of years, and its earth has yielded treasures speaking eloquently of contacts with the Minoan, Greek, and Roman cultures. But the Golden Age arrived in the 12th century, when Visby and Gotland dominated the trade of northern and western Europe and the town could undoubtedly be classed as one of the major cities of the world. Wealth followed wealth, and within the confines of the city wall alone, itself a magnificent structure from every standpoint, the rich merchants erected no less than 17 churches. Outside of the city, farmer-merchants built parish churches more like small cathedrals than rural houses of worship.

Trade routes shifted. War parties ravaged. The first of a series of major catastrophes took place in 1361, when the island and city fell to Danish King Valdemar Atterdag. The decline had set in with a vengeance. The island was variously occupied by Baltic powers during the succeeding century and more, until 1645, when it was definitely sealed into the Swedish kingdom.

Exploring Gotland

Today, the island is a vacation paradise *par excellence.* There is no lack of sights in the traditional meaning. See the churches and medieval merchant palaces of Visby—St. Nicholas, St. Clemens, the Church of the Holy Spirit, St. Catarina, and a half dozen more—and the wall. *Walk* to see Visby—pick up a map and an English guidebook at the travel bureau in Burmeister House, itself a historic building near the harbor—and wander. Wherever you go, you can't go wrong. Don't miss the museum, Fornsalen, particularly the impressive picture stones, which antedate the Viking rune stones. There are other remarkable finds on display, too—coins and jewelry from many centuries, religious art (note particularly the gentle loveliness of the Öja Madonna, a medieval wood scuplture), and ancient weapons unearthed from the scenes of battles for this once flourishing island.

If you happen to be in Visby at the end of July or in early August don't miss the pageant opera "Petrus de Dacia" performed every year in the ruin of St. Nicolai Church.

Justice cannot be done to the cultural history of Visby and Gotland in anything smaller than a complete book. The names of the masters who designed and decorated these churches have been lost to history, but scientists have been able to identify and classify a few of them by characteristic features of their styles as they recur in various works. Although Visby is hilly and there are cobbled stones on the streets, you should take the time to walk leisurely around the city. Car traffic is restricted here.

The stalactite caves at Lummelunda are unique in this part of the world and are worth visiting, as is the Krusmyntagarden (herb garden), north of Visby, close to the sea.

Although many tourists rent bicycles for tours of the island, there are cars for rent and there is a good network of buses. The Tourist Office arranges many day tours by bus—call and ask for details. It should be noted that the island of Fårö and the northeast corner of Gotland itself are restricted areas for foreigners.

The Local Churches

On the whole island, which measures only about 48 kilometers (30 miles) by 128 kilometers (80 miles), there are approximately 100 churches still intact and in use today, dating from Gotland's great commercial area. Among them are:

Barlingbro, dating from the 13th century, with vault paintings, stained glass windows, remarkable 12th-century font.

Dalhem, one of the 16 largest rural religious edifices, construction begun about 1200 or somewhat earlier, an exquisite example of Gotland church architecture.

Gothem, one of Gotland's most impressive country churches, mainly built during the 13th century, with notable series of paintings of that period.

Grötlingbo, a 14th-century church with stone sculpture and stained glass: note the 12th century reliefs on the façade.

Tingstäde, another of the 16 largest, a puzzle of six building periods from 1169 to 1300 or so. Note the general proportions, the stained-glass windows, and murals from the 14th century.

Roma Cloister Church, the massive ruins from a Cistercian monastery founded in 1164. The ruins are sufficiently well preserved to give a good picture of the architecture and contruction.

Öja, decorated with paintings and containing a famous Holy Rood from the late 13th century.

Island Bird Refuges

There are a number of other sights well worth your time. Among them are curious rock formations along the coasts, including the "Old Man of Hoburgen" at the southern tip of the island; and two island bird refuges off the coast south of Visby, Stora and Lilla Karlsö. The bird population consists to a large extent of guillemots, which look like penguins. Visits to these refuges are permitted only in company with a recognized guide, and the easiest way to see them is to join a conducted tour from Visby.

PRACTICAL INFORMATION FOR GOTLAND

TOURIST INFORMATION. There are tourist offices at: Burmeisterska Huset, Visby (0498-109 82), open April through September, and the ferry terminal (0498-470 65).

TELEPHONE CODES. We give telephone codes in the hotel and restaurant lists that follow. These codes need only be used when calling from outside the area concerned.

HOTELS AND RESTAURANTS. *Snäck* (E), (0498-600 00). 102 rooms. Between airport and Visby. All rooms face west. Excellent restaurant, nightclub. Beach, pool, sauna, canoes. Airport bus. AE, DC, MC, V. *Visby Hotel* (M), Strandgatan 6 (0498-119 25). 92 rooms. Central, airport bus. Restaurant, *Oskar* nightclub. AE, MC, V. *Villa Borgen* (M), Adelsgatan 11 (0498-71170). 18 rooms. Breakfast only. Family-run. MC. *Solhem* (I), (0498-790 70). 80 rooms. Central. On two floors. Restaurant, dancing. MC. *Toftagården* (I), Tofta (0498-654 00). 69 rooms. 300 meters (about 300 yards) from beach. Restaurant, windsurfing, billiards. MC.

Restaurants. *Jacob Dubbe,* Strandgatan 16 (0495-497 22). International menu. In medieval building. Open 22 hours a day. *Rosengården,* Stora Torget (0495-181 90). Close to cloister ruin. Italian and French cuisine. Open-air service in garden. Charming. MC. *Värdshuset* (Inn), Lindgården, Strandgatan 26 (0495-187 00). In old building. Excellent food. MC

Youth Hostels. For bookings and information about youth hostels on the island of Gotland, call 0498-912 20. *Visby,* Gråboskolan (0498-169 33). Central. Open May 31 to Aug. 3.

Camping. There are many three-star sites on the island. Try *Kneippbyn* (0498-643 65). On the beach four km. (2½ miles) south of Visby. 20 cottages for rent.

HOW TO GET AROUND. One way, but not the least expensive, to see the archipelago is by chartered cruiser (Taxi-Båt). In summer scheduled water-bus services ply to most points of the archipelago from Stockholm: *embarking* at Klara Strand (near City Hall) for Gripsholm Castle and Drottningholm Castle; at Munkbron (Old Town) for Skokloster Castle; at Strömkajen (near Grand Hotel) for Sandhamn, Husarö, Möja and Vaxholm; at Slussen for Sandhamn (bus with boat connection); from Central Station by train, bus and coach to Utö.

It takes only 40 minutes to fly from Stockholm to Visby—the airport is three km. (about two miles) from the city. There are also day or night trips from the port of Nynäshamn (one hour by train, bus or car from Stockholm). You can leave Stockholm in the evening and return by midnight the next day. The boats on this run carry cars. There are also ferries from Västervik and Oskarshamn.

Gotland is an ideal island for a bicycling holiday. There are over 4,000 bicycles for rent and the tourist office will sell you complete bike "packages." Gotland has a tourist office at Norrmalmstorg in Stockholm.

PLACES TO VISIT. In the archipelago. The castles at Vaxholm and Tyresö. In the valley of Lake Mälar: Gripsholm Castle and its portrait gallery, the 17th-century castle (with its Motor Museum) of Skokloster, Sigtuna, with its rune stones and House of Antiquities.

GOTLAND. Fornsalen (Gotland Historical Museum). At Strandgatan 12. It features graves from the Stone, Bronze and Iron Ages. Also picture stones and hoards from Viking times, ecclesiastical art. Open Tues. to Sun 1–3; closed Mon.; May 15 to Aug 15, daily 11–5.

Krusmyntagården. Herb garden, two km. (1.2 miles) south of Lummelundagrottorna Caves, near the sea. 300 different herbs; also herbs for sale. On Tues. and Thurs. nights, entertainers (from Gotland) and *asado* (barbecue). Open mid-June to Aug., daily 9–6. For information call 0498-701 53.

Lummelundagrottorna. 13 km. (nine miles) north of Visby. Ancient limestone caves with stalactites. 300-meter (984-foot) long cave with smaller and larger caves 6–8 meters (19–26 feet) high. Guided tours continuously. Souvenir shop and cafeteria. Open May to Sept., 9–4 daily (Jun. 21 to Aug. 9, 9–7 daily). For information call 0498-730 50.

SWEDEN'S SOUTHLAND

Breadbasket, Battlefield and Summer
Playground

Southern Sweden is a world of its own, clearly distinguished from the rest of Sweden by its geography, culture, and history.

Skåne (pronounced "scorner"), the southernmost province, is known as the "granary of Sweden." It occupies a more or less rectangular area, including the almost square peninsula that forms the southern tip of the country and supports no less than one-eighth of the whole Swedish population. It is a comparatively small province of beautifully fertile plains, sand beaches, scores of castles and châteaux, thriving farms, medieval churches, and summer resorts.

East of the northern end of Skåne is the province of Blekinge, called "Sweden's garden," occupying another southern coastal reach extending to the east coast. North of the western part of Skåne, ranging along the west coast of Sweden, is the province of Halland, a rolling country of heaths and ridges rising above the beaches. Halland faces the Kattegat (the southeastern part of the North Sea), and contributed its full share of the Viking forces which once struck terror into the populations of many countries. It still produces its share of modern sea captains.

There is an old tradition that while the Lord was busy making Ska °ne into the fertile garden that it is today, the devil sneaked past him farther north, and made the province of Småland. The result was harsh, unyielding, unfriendly country of stone and woods. When the Lord caught up with Satan and saw what had happened he said, "All right, it's too late to do anything about the land . . . so I'm going to make the people." He did, and He made them so tough and stubborn and resilient and long-lived that they carved a true civilization out of their sparse heritage. There is still a folk saying that you can deposit a son of the province of Småland on a barren stone island with only an ax in his hands and he'll manage—and have a garden going before long.

Whatever the validity of the legend, it is true that Småland is vastly different from the other three provinces of southern Sweden. It is a good deal larger and is noted particularly for its glass industries, as well as furniture and other wood products, and its great historic region with Kalmar at the center.

Skåne, Blekinge, and Halland (Halland is described in the *West Coast* chapter) also form a natural historical group of provinces; they were actually the last incorporations of territory into what constitutes the present-day Swedish kingdom. The time was 1658. These southern provinces had been part of Denmark for centuries (and thus the medieval architecture is Danish). Sweden and Denmark had been fighting intermittently for generations. Karl X (anglicized as Charles X), a king and general of parts, whatever his faults, was off in Poland on one of the many indecisive Swedish attempts for a reckoning with that country. This looked to the Danes like a perfect opportunity for a reckoning with the Swedes. But when the Danish fleet arrived at Danzig to fall on the Swedish rear, the Swedes were moving overland at top speed toward Denmark. After two bold, unprecedented marches across the ice of the sounds separating the Danish islands, the Swedish army of 12,000 battle-hardened men faced an almost undefended Copenhagen. Although Sweden was also at war with Poland and Russia, Karl X was in a position almost to name his own terms. They were so rough that one of the Danish commissioners, preparing to sign this historic Peace of Roskilde, complained, "If only I didn't know how to write!".

By virtue of that treaty Sweden achieved natural southern boundaries—the coasts of the Baltic Sea—for the first time in its history, and acquired the rich territory which now nurtures one-fourth of the population. But the marks of long association with Denmark and its Continental culture live on in the language, the architecture, the way of life and the gastronomy.

Exploring Helsingborg

Let's say that you have arrived in Helsingborg from the Danish side by ferry. In front of you stretches a long, comparatively narrow square, dominated at the far end, on the height, by a medieval tower stronghold known as Kärnan (the Keep). The surviving center tower, built to provide living quarters and defend the medieval castle of Helsingborg, is the most remarkable relic of its kind in the north. The interior, which may be visited, is divided into several floors, containing medieval kitchen fittings, a chapel, etc. From the top you have a magnificent view of the coast, the Sound, and the Danish shore.

A thousand years ago, this city was an important European capital. Today it is a thriving industrial town of some 101,000 inhabitants, the eighth largest city in Sweden. For centuries Helsingborg and its Danish neighbor across the Sound, Elsinore (Helsingør), only about five kilometers (three miles) away, controlled all shipping traffic in and out of the Baltic Sea. There is a train and ferry terminal here for services between Sweden and Denmark, with a sailing every 20 minutes.

In Södra Storgatan are St. Mary's Church, built in the 13th century and rebuilt during the 15th century, with an interesting triptych and magnificent late Renaissance pulpit, and the Town Museum, containing exhibits depicting the early history of Helsingborg. Take time to visit Fredriksdals Friluftmuseum, an 18th-century mansion set in a lovely old park around which old Skåne farmhouses and buildings have been set up to form an open-air museum. During summer there are performances in the attractive open-air theater.

About five kilometers (three miles) north of the city—bus to Pålsjöbaden, then a half-hour walk along the Sound—is Sofiero Castle, summer residence of the late King, built in 1865 in Dutch Renaissance style. The grounds are open to the public (enter by northern gate near gardener's lodge).

Golf and Tennis in Båstad

If you proceed north from Helsingborg, you come immediately into a region of summer resorts stretching along a promontory. One of the main resort towns is Mölle, near the end of the peninsula, which looks out upon the south end of the Kattegat. Proceeding back along the north shore of this peninsula, you arrive in Ängelholm, a small and charming city at least 500 years old, which has become a popular summer resort. Here you can see Sweden's oldest local prison—now a museum.

Only some of the main stops can be mentioned here. As you continue north along the coast, the next in line will be Båstad, perhaps the most fashionable of the summer resorts in this region. It is frequented throughout the summer by the international set, and ambassadors and ministers of several countries may sometimes be in residence there at the same time. The principal attractions include the natural beauty of the region (known for its flowers and fruit orchards), 18-hole golf course, and several tennis courts. International tennis tournaments are held every year at the beginning of July.

Recommended is a visit to the Norrviken Gardens, three kilometers (two miles) northwest of Båstad. They comprise a number of gardens of various styles, agreeably laid out in varied grounds and each one in character with the landscape's lines, perspectives and vistas. Just east of Båstad is Malen, with an interesting sepulchral mound from the 11th century B.C. It has been excavated and restored so that you can enter and study the stones set up in the form of a ship. Also here are a 15th-century church and many old houses in picturesque narrow winding streets.

Don't miss Torekov, a little fishing village on the point of a peninsula about nine kilometers (six miles) due west of Båstad, which has many summer visitors. Despite a too generous influx of summer folks in July and August, many of whom have built or bought their own homes, the community remains an authentic part of this coastal region. There is a tiny but interesting museum—not a few of whose treasures have been gathered from ships wrecked in the treacherous waters off the point. The days here are serene and rhythmical with the pulse of an ancient way of life, a life close to the sea. Just off the coast is an island—Hallands Väderö—a national reserve known for its flora and bird life.

Continuing north from Båstad, you cross almost at once into Halland, another of the provinces acquired by Sweden in the fantastically profitable peace of 1658. By this time you will have noticed the changing nature of the landscape, the way ridges billow up in more pronounced fashion from the coast. In back of them are broad heaths unique to this part of Sweden.

Malmö—Third Largest City

If you start south from Helsingborg, the first coastal town of any size will be Landskrona, a modern industrial and shipping center with some 35,000 inhabitants. The 17th-century fortifications surrounding Landskrona Castle are reputed to be the best preserved relics of their kind in Europe. The citadel was built in 1549. From Landskrona there are boats to the beautiful island of Ven, between Sweden and Denmark.

Malmö, with a population of 235,000, is the small but opulent capital of a small but opulent province and a sense of well-being strikes you upon arrival. It has the friendly atmosphere normally associated with much smaller places, and its coastal location close to Denmark has given it a more cosmopolitan atmosphere than most other Swedish towns. This is reflected in its tremendous variety of restaurants— Greek, Italian and so on—and there are actually reputed to be more restaurants per head than any other Swedish city, including Stockholm. Malmö even has Sweden's only mosque. There are many reminders here of the great trading days of the Hanseatic League. The Rådhuset (Court House) dates back to the 16th century and the Malmöhus Castle, now a museum, to the 16th century. Nearby is the Malmö Technical Museum. The Lilla Torg, an attractive small cobblestoned square, has buildings from the 17th and 18th centuries, which have been restored over the past 20 years.

The impressive statue on the central square is that of Karl X—the king who acquired this part of the country for Sweden. Just off the square (look for the steeple and follow your eyes) you will find St. Peter's Church, a brick structure from shortly after 1300. It is the largest Gothic church in south Sweden.

In addition to the usual historical sights offered by most Swedish cities, Malmö distinguishes itself by having also a top-flight modern one—the City Theater. It is surprising that this comparatively small city has been able to build and maintain such an imposing stage. It was completed in 1944 and seats 1,700 persons. The city also now has an impressive new 1,300-seat concert hall (Konserthuset), which has provided the Malmö Symphony Orchestra with its first permanent home in its 60-year-old history. The concert season runs between September and May. The Malmö-card gives you free transportation and free or reduced entrance to various attractions, as well as convenient sightseeing. Buy it at the airport, railway station or tourist office.

The University City of Lund

Less than 30 kilometers (19 miles) northeast of Malmö, connected by frequent bus and train services, is Lund. Lund was once the religious capital of a region which stretched from Iceland to Finland, over which the Roman Catholic archbishop resident here held more or less absolute sway in matters of faith. The city was founded almost a thousand years ago by the Danish King Canute the Great, and during its early

of the country, while the northern part gives a hint of the rocks and woods of Småland across the border. Blekinge, like Skåne and Halland, shares a long association with Denmark.

Sölvesborg, according to legend, was founded in A.D. 700 by a sea-going king named Sölve. Today it is a small port supported also by industry. The principal sights are the old castle, which played an important part in the Swedish-Danish feuds, and the church begun in the 13th century and constructed in Gothic style.

In Listerlandet, near Hällevik, there are several picturesque fishing villages. It also boasts a small fishing museum, with relics of fishing from long ago. The ferry from Nogersund will take you to Hanö, with one of the tallest lighthouses in Northern Europe.

At the Salmon Aquarium at Mörrum you can see salmon and trout in their natural environment. The King and his guests gather at Mörrum around April 1 each year to open the salmon-fishing season. Mörrum's river has a world-wide reputation for salmon fishing. It was here that the world's biggest sea-trout was caught—32.3 lb. Salmon up to 44 lb. are not uncommon here.

Karlshamn, a port which accommodates ocean-going vessels, is an idyllic coastal town. The Kastellet, or fortress, overlooking the channel into the harbor, was started by Karl X to defend the province of Blekinge from the Danes, who had just yielded it up to him. The elevators for grains and oilseeds are said to be the largest such concentration in Europe. The emigrants' monument "Karl-Oskar and Kristina" commemorates the great Swedish exodus to America. There is a replica of this moving monument in Lindstrom Square, Minnesota. The boat trips to the Kastellet in the harbor, and from Järnavik to the beautiful island of Tjärö are to be recommended.

Ronneby was well known to vacationers of a couple of generations past for its mineral wells. The rebuilt resort hotel is set in an unusually beautiful park. The principal sight is the fortress church, Heliga Korsets Kyrka (Holy Cross Church), dating from the 12th century.

Karlskrona, a city founded in the 17th century, is built on 30 islands. It is an important naval base and acquired some notoriety a few years ago when a Soviet submarine ran aground at the entrance to the harbor after having been the victim of a "navigation error." At the Varvsmuseet (Marine Museum), there is an excellent collection of figureheads, model ships and much more. It is one of the finest marine museums in the world. Here in Karlskrona is Sweden's oldest wooden church, Amiralitetskyrkan, with its poor-box, Rosenbom, outside. Two churches here, the Holy Trinity and Fredrik's, were designed by the outstanding architect Nicodemus Tessin. The Kungsholmens Fortress, built around 1680, was erected to protect the harbor. Another fortress dating from the same time, the Drottningskärs Kastell on the island of Aspö, is still intact.

Historic Kalmar

Kalmar has the distinction of a mention on a rune stone from the 11th century. The oldest part of its famous castle dates back to the 12th century. You can see at a glance why Kalmar was once called "the Lock and Key of Sweden," and 'why it played an historic role in Scandinavian history before the airplane added a third dimension to warfare. The magnificent Renaissance castle—the earliest parts of which date from the 12th century—was also a mighty fortress, dominating the sound which separates the mainland from the island of Öland. When Kalmar began its age of greatness, the southern border of Sweden was only a few kilometers south—on the then Danish province of Blekinge. The long narrow island lying parallel to the mainland and thus forming a narrow channel completed the strategic picture: whoever controlled Kalmar controlled traffic along the coast north to Stockholm.

The importance of Kalmar is reflected in the name Kalmar Union (an agreement signed here in 1397), an ill-starred attempt to unite Scandinavia under one ruler. It limped along for more than a century of intermittent civil wars before it was formally dissolved by Swedish independence under Gustav Vasa in 1523. It was this great king who made Kalmar Castle with its courts and battlements, its moat, its round towers. But even this powerful stronghold could not prevent the destruction and ravaging of the city in the recurring Danish-Swedish wars. The city was practically wiped out in the so-called Kalmar War of 1611–13. Fire again destroyed the town in 1647, and, with the Peace of Roskilde, the region lost some of its strategic importance. The decline had begun. Today Kalmar is the commercial and administrative center for southeastern Småland, a port and tourist attraction.

The principal sight is, of course, the castle. (*Note:* it closes at 4 P.M.) You get a good picture of the integrated life of a whole royal establishment as it functioned centuries ago, from the king's bedroom to the huge kitchens. Note especially the Castle Chapel, a charming little place of worship in rococo and Renaissance, which is still used for divine services (Sundays at 10 A.M.). The grim dungeon is a curiosity —it was cunningly placed below the surface level of the nearby sea— thus making attempts to tunnel out impossible. Prisoners sometimes survived for years in this dingy, damp hole. The castle also contains the extensive collections of the Kalmar Museum. One of the major attractions of the museum is the exhibition of some of the results of the salvage operation on the Swedish man-of-war *Kronan* (the Crown), which sank in battle with the Danish–Dutch fleet in June 1676, off the southeast coast of Öland with the loss of 800 lives. The wreck was discovered only in 1980 but has yielded some rich archeological finds, including valuable coins, bottles containing 300-year-old brandy and an officer's personal casket with his complete navigational outfit.

You will find the city itself rich in atmosphere and structures from the 17th and 18th centuries, when the present city was largely laid out and constructed. In particular see the cathedral (designed by Nicodemus Tessin the Elder and built about 1675). Not far from here is a smaller square (Lilla Torget), with the residence of the provincial governor, originally from 1674. The French King Louis XVIII lived here briefly in exile shortly after 1800.

Windmills and Rune Stones on Öland

The island of Öland is reached from Kalmar by a 6,070-meter (almost four miles) bridge, the longest in Europe. There are many rune stones here, dating from the Viking era. There are also relics from the Iron Age in the many graves and 16 fortifications on the island.

Gråborg Fortress, probably dating from about A.D. 500, must have been gigantic at one time, for the walls enclose an area some 229 meters (250 yards) long and 174 meters (190 yards) wide. Now only the massive stone walls, as much as eight meters (25 feet) high and eight meters (25 feet) thick, remain of this onetime stronghold.

Probably the most interesting site is at Eketorp—an excavated fortified village which has been restored to give visitors an impression of what life must have been like in a 5th-century community.

Borgholm Castle ruin is perhaps the biggest and most beautiful ruin of a castle stronghold in Sweden. It originated as a medieval fortress, was rebuilt during the 16th and 17th centuries, and ravaged by fire in 1806. It overlooks the city of Borgholm from a commanding site and is most impressive by moonlight.

Solliden is the summer residence of the royal family. The beautiful grounds around the sparkling white mansion are open from June through Aug., 12 noon–2 P.M., and are located on the outskirts of Borgholm, within easy walking distance.

The landscape of Öland is so different from the mainland that you feel almost as though you had entered another country. This, and a great profusion of old-fashioned, more or less Dutch-type windmills, give the island an unmistakable profile. With luck you may be able to count as many as 54 of the 400 windmills in a couple of hours' auto tour.

Much of Öland is covered by a huge, treeless steppe known as the Alvar, a limestone plateau without counterpart in northern Europe. It gives a sense of peace bordering on quiet desolation. During spring and fall, this is the place to watch the migratory birds. Hundreds of species rest up here from their long flights. On the southern tip of the island, at Ottenby, is a bird station and an old lighthouse, Långe Jan (Long John), from which there is a magnificent view.

A Kingdom of Glass

In Kalmar or Växjö you are only an hour or two from some of the finest glass works in the world—Orrefors, Kosta, Boda, Strömbergshyttan. Exquisite pieces by famed designers from these factories are found in exclusive shops almost all over the world. But don't look for something that resembles an industrial region. The plants are scattered in the wooded wilderness of Småland, communities of a few hundred people built around the factory. From these isolated, unprepossessing villages go regular shipments to London and Paris, New York's Fifth Avenue, the cities of South America; special orders start on their way addressed to kings and emperors, presidents and ministers, tycoons and simple lovers of beautiful things. The glassblowers show off their skills every weekday, but they start work at 6 A.M. and finish at 3 P.M., so a morning visit is advisable. Inquire at local tourist offices to be sure of times.

You can now visit most of the major plants to see the glassblowers at work and they all have large shops, some of supermarket size, where you can pick up remarkable bargains from the "seconds" on display. You'll probably be hard put to it to discover any faults on most items, but if you want to be sure of buying a "perfect" product you'll have to do your buying in a normal shop. Even so, you will probably save substantially in comparison with prices in other countries.

Orrefors is the best-known Swedish glass maker, probably produces the greatest variety, and the quality and design are, of course, unsurpassed. The community of Orrefors is located about an hour west and a little north of Kalmar (train connections). It's so unpretentious you'll pass right through it if you're not looking.

Watching the skilled craftsmen of Orrefors is almost like a slow dance—with the pieces of red hot glass being carried back and forth, passed from hand to hand, as they are blown and shaped by trained, sensitive muscles. The basic procedure and the tools are said not to have changed appreciably in 2,000 years. The designing and engraving processes are also fascinating—and the finished product is the result of unusual teamwork, from the designer to the craftsman to the finisher. (Many of the pieces get no further treatment after leaving the blower and shaper, however.) One of the special attractions of Orrefors is a magnificent display of various pieces made through the years, ranging in value up to thousands of kronor.

Other glassworks are: Johansfors, with a Crystal Museum showing a complete collection from the beginning of this century; Kosta, with a museum and exhibition hall. There are local glass museums at Lindshammar, Pukeberg, Rosdala and Skruf. The largest glass museum in Northern Europe is in Växjö, in the Småland Museum.

Tracing the Emigrants

There are about ten million Americans with Scandinavian blood. Of the Swedes, most came from Småland and the island of Öland. The emigration started in the middle of the last century and continued until the last war. On Öland, for instance, practically every household has someone who has been in America for a couple of years. Many come back, and nearly a fifth of the population, or 5,000 people, have lived and worked in America. Strangely enough, the people never traveled elsewhere to any extent. Some have seen Denmark and England en route to or from the States, others saw something of France, courtesy of the American Army in World War II. The story of the early Swedish emigrants to the U.S. has been masterfully told by a Swedish author, Vilhelm Moberg, in *The Emigrants, Unto a Good Land* and *Last Letter Home,* published, and made into a film, in English. It deals with a family from the mainland, only a few miles from Kalmar, and a look at it will give you an interesting sidelight on the histories of Sweden and America.

In Långasjö there is a small wooden house called Klasatorp open to visitors in the summer months. This was an emigrant's home, and the people here wear the costume of former days and work the farm in the traditional manner. The following tour is suggested for those who wish to see the land of their forefathers: Hovmantorp–Kosta–Ljuder–Algotsboda–Rävemåla–Linnerud–Ingelstad–Växjö. This tour covers a distance of 155 kilometers or 96 miles.

In Växjö the Emigrant Institute has an exhibition telling the story of the "American Dream" and the emigrants. There is also a research center here where the names of most emigrants are kept on file and many American visitors come here each year to trace their ancestors. In August Minnesota Day is celebrated in front of the Emigrant Institute.

PRACTICAL INFORMATION FOR SWEDEN'S SOUTHLAND

TOURIST INFORMATION. The region's tourist offices may be found at the following places: **Ängelholm,** Storgatan 21 (0431–163 50). **Eksjö,** Österlånggatan 31 (0381 –133 05). **Helsingborg,** Rådhuset (042–12 03 10). **Jönköping,** V. Storgatan 9 (036–16 90 50). **Kalmar,** Larmgatan 6 (0480–153 50). **Karlskrona,** S. Smedjegatan 6 (0455–834 90). **Lund,** St. Petri Kyrkogatan 4 (046–12 45 90). **Malmö,** Hamngatan 1 (040–34 12 70). **Ronneby,** Snäckebacksplan (0457–176 50). **Västervik,** Strömsholmen (0490–136 95). **Växjö,** Kronobergsgatan 8 (0470–41410). **Ystad,** St. Knuts Torg (0411–772 90).

The **Malmö card,** costing about SEK 65 for three days and SEK 95 for a week, offers free bus transport in the Malmö area, free entrance to museums, and discounts on such things as restaurants, sightseeing and souvenirs in shops. Children half price.

TELEPHONE CODES. We have given telephone codes for all the towns and villages in the hotel and restaurant lists that follow. These codes need only be used when calling from outside the town or village concerned.

HOTELS AND RESTAURANTS. Because of its many tourist attractions and the popularity of its summer holiday resorts, this region is one of Sweden's best equipped from the point of view of hotel accommodations. Remember, too, that resort hotels have advantageous pension rates for stays of three days or longer.

A special hotel package is available at 21 hotels in Malmö daily from June 19 through Aug. 23, over the Christmas and Easter periods, and at weekends only for the rest of the year. Prices per person vary from SEK 160 to SEK 300 (double occupancy) and the package includes breakfast and the Malmö card (described above). Children under 15 qualify for a 50% rebate, for which they also get breakfast and the Malmö card. The package can be booked through travel agents or direct by telephone (040–34 12 68).

For fine provincial cuisine—salmon and eel dishes are a specialty—in an authentic atmosphere, stop at some of the old country inns for a meal or two. The word for inn is *Gästgivaregård.* Here you often find *Smörgåbords* with up to 150 dishes, such as pickled herring, shrimp, patés, home-made pies etc. To finish, ask for *spettekaka,* a delicious cake baked with eggs and plenty of sugar. Apart from those restaurants listed below, most of the region's restaurants will be found in the hotels themselves—see the listings.

ÄNGELHOLM. *Lilton* (I), Järnvägsgatan 29 (0431–824 00). 14 rooms. Central, near railway station. Breakfast only. AE, MC, V.

BÄCKASKOG. *Bäckaskogs Slott* (M), (044–532 50). 49 rooms. 12 km. (seven miles) from Kristianstad. Castle from 13th century, formerly a monastery. Unique atmosphere. Bus. Rowboats and bikes for rent. AE, DC, MC, V.

BÅSTAD. *Hemmeslövs Herrgårdspensionat* (Manor House) (I) (0431–700 32). 124 rooms. Pension. Restaurant, dancing. Sauna, heated outdoor pool, tennis, 1.5 km. (a mile) to beach. Open Easter to Sept. plus weekends. AE, V. *Hotel Pension Enehall* (I) (0431–750 15). 75 rooms. Pension. Restaurant, cafeteria. Sauna, outdoor pool nearby, 400 meters (440 yards) to beach. AE, DC, MC, V.

BODA. Youth Hostel. *Boda Glassworks* (0481–242 30). 49 beds. Outdoor pool. Bus from Nybro. Open all year.

BORGHOLM. (On the island of **Öland**). *Halltorps Gästgiveri* (Inn) (M), nine km. (five miles) south of Borgholm (0485–552 50). 10 rooms. Manor house from 17th century. Pension. Known for excellent food. Closed Jan. to Feb. AE, DC, MC, V.

EKSJÖ. *Stadshotellet* (I), Stora Torget 5 (0381–130 20). 36 rooms. Central, 500 meters (546 yards) from railway station. Pension, restaurant, dancing. Also vegetarian food. Street with best-preserved 17th-century low wooden houses in the country. AE, DC, MC, V.
Youth Hostel. At Eksjö Museum, Österlånggatan 31 (0381–119 91). 50 beds. Central. Open late May through Aug.

GRÄNNA. *Scandic Hotel Gyllene Uttern* (M), (0390–108 00). 53 rooms. Attractive modern-style manor house with its own wedding chapel and baronial-style dining room.

HELSINGBORG. *Grand Hotel* (E), Stortorget 8 (042–12 01 70). 130 rooms. Air terminal, 200 meters (220 yards) to railway and ferries to Denmark. Restaurant in English style, cocktail bar, sauna. AE, DC, MC, V. *Högvakten* (the Guardhouse) (I), Stortorget 14 (042–12 03 90). 46 rooms. Restaurant, sauna. AE, DC, MC, V.
Youth Hostel. *Villa Thalassa*, Dag Hammarskjöldsväg (042–11 03 84). 134 beds. Wonderful view of the sea. Open year-round.

HÖÖR. *Frostavallen* (I), (0413–220 60). 93 rooms. Cafeteria. Solarium. Canoes, bikes for rent.

KALMAR. *Stadshotellet* (E), Stortorget 14 (0480–151 80). 150 rooms. Restaurant, sauna, rooms for disabled or allergy-sufferers. AE, DC, MC, V. *Witt* (E), S. Långgatan 42 (0480–152 50), 112 rooms. Restaurant, cocktail bar, pub, dancing. Sauna, pool, airport bus. AE, DC, MC, V. *Slottshotellet* (M), Slottsvägen 7 (0480–882 60). 29 rooms. Elegant town house, near the park, 500 meters (546 yards) from town center, view of the bay. Sauna. Breakfast only. AE, DC, MC, V.

KARLSHAMN. *Scandic* (M), Jannebergsvägen 2 (0454–166 60). 94 rooms. Motor hotel. Restaurant, sauna. AE, DC, MC, V.

KARLSKRONA. *Statt Hotel* (E), Ronnebygatan 37 (0455–192 50). Central. Restaurant, nightclub. AE, DC, MC, V.
Restaurants. *Krutviken* (M), Wämö, three km. (two miles) from the town center (0455–115 37). In park with a fine view of sea. Fish menu. In winter open 1–6 P.M. only. In summer open in evenings also. Closed Mon. MC, V. *Skeppet* (the Ship) (M), N. Kungsgatan 1 (0455–103 71). Marine atmosphere overlooking the main square. Fish dishes a specialty. Has pub section—*Jollen.* Closed Sat. and Sun. MC, V.

LÅNGASJÖ. Youth Hostel. 65 km. (40 miles) from Kalmar, near the glassworks (0477–503 10). 53 beds. Many emigrants to America came from this area. Rowboats and bikes for rent. Open year-round.

LUND. *Grand* (E), Bantorget 1 (046–11 70 10). 87 rooms. Central. Restaurant, also vegetarian menu. AE, DC, MC, V. *Sparta* (I), Tunavägen 39 (046–12 40 80). 150 rooms. Pension, restaurant, sauna. AE, MC, V.

MALMÖ. *Savoy* (L), Norra Vallgatan 62 (040–702 30). 100 rooms. Central. Restaurants, nightclub. AE, DC, MC, V. *Garden* (E), Baltzarsgatan 20 (040–10 40 00). 173 rooms. Central, in shopping district, close to airport bus. *Noble House* (E), Gustav Adolfstorg 47 (040–10 15 00). 128 rooms. Opened in 1986 in central but quiet location. Restaurant, rooms suitable for handicapped guests. AE, DC, MC, V. *St. Jörgen* (E), Stora Nygatan 35 (040–773 00). 285 rooms. In the heart of Malmö, five or ten minutes' walk to airport bus, rail station and harbor. *Tahonga Bar,* self-service salad bar. AE, DC, MC, V. *Scandic Crown* (M), Amiralsgatan 19 (040–10 07 30). 154 rooms. Central, in same complex as new concert hall. Restaurant, sauna, swimming pool, rooms for handicapped guests. AE, DC, MC, V. *Skyline* (M), Stadiongatan at Exhibition Halls (040–803 00). 270 rooms. Luxury accommodation at moderate cost. Restaurant, sauna. AE, DC, MC, V.

Astoria (M), Gråbrödersgatan 7 (040–786 60). 30 rooms. In old city, close to railways, airport bus and ferries. A fine family-run hotel. MC, V. *Baltzar* (M), Södergatan 20 (040–720 05). 41 rooms. Central location, on pedestrian shopping street. AE, DC, MC, V. *Strand* (I), Strandgatan 50 (040–16 20 30). 23 rooms. Quiet, near ferry Limhamn to Dragør. Breakfast. AE, MC.

Restaurants. *Översten* (E), Regementsgatan 52A (040–91 91 00). The tallest building in the area—26 stories above Malmö. Fantastic view with the Danish coast on the horizon. AE, MC, V. *Pers Krog* (E), Limhamnsvägen 2 (040–670 11). One of the best restaurants in town, renowned for seafood specialties. AE, DC, MC, V. *Kockska Krogen* (E), Frans Suellsgatan 3 (040–703 20). Historic cellar restaurant, part of a building dating back to 1525. AE, DC, MC, V. *Rådhuskällaren* (M), Stortorget (040–790 20). Popular establishment in cellars below the City Hall. AE, DC, MC, V. *Fågel Fenix* (M), Isak Slaktaregatan 6 (040–11 10 59). Excellent vegetarian restaurant. MC. *Falstaff* (M), Baltzarsgatan 25 (040–11 40 09). Steak-house with sauna on the premises. AE, DC, MC, V. *Centralens* (I), at central railway station (040–766 80). Good value for money, with popular salad buffet and special dish of the day. AE, DC, MC, V.

Youth Hostel. *Södergården,* Backavägen 18 (040–822 20). 174 beds. Bus 36 from Central Station to "Vandrarhemmet." Sauna. Open Feb. through Nov.

MÖRRUM. *Walhalla* (I), Stationsvägen 24 (0454–500 44). 25 rooms. Three km. (two miles) to beach on the Baltic. Pension, restaurant. Salmon fishing. AE, MC, V.

OTTENBY. Youth Hostel. (On the island of Öland.) Near Ås Church on the southern tip of the island, three km. (two miles) from Ottenby Kungsgård (0485–620 62). 96 beds. Open year-round.

RONNEBY. *Ronneby Brunn* (M) (0457–127 50). 301 rooms. Pension, restaurant, dancing, nightclub. Sauna, heated outdoor pool in summer, tennis, minigolf. Airport bus. AE, DC, MC, V.

TOFTAHOLM. *Toftaholm Herrgårdshotel* (M), (0370–440 55). 40 rooms. On the shore of Lake Vidöstern. Manor house dating back to 14th century, claimed to have a resident ghost. Excellent home cooking. AE, DC, MC, V.

VÄXJÖ. *Royal Corner* (L), Lidbergsgatan 11 (0470–100 00). 165 rooms. Restaurant, piano-bar, pool, sauna. Free parking. *Statt* (M), Kungsgatan (0470–134 00). 139 rooms. Restaurant, dancing, *Gyllene Oxen Pub, Lucky Swede Bar,* honoring a golddigger in the Klondike. Whirlpool, sauna, solarium. Airport bus. 200 meters (220 yards) to rail station. AE, DC, MC, V.

Restaurant. *Teaterkällaren* (M), Nygatan 26 (0470–255 41). Central. Fish is the specialty. MC, V.

Youth Hostel. *Evedal,* three km. (two miles) from road 23, six km. (four miles) northeast of Växjö (0470–630 70). 55 beds. Closed mid-Dec. to mid-Jan. Direct bus to Växjö in summer.

YSTAD. *Ystads Saltsjöbad* (Salt-Sea Bath) (M) (0411–136 30). 110 rooms. On the beach, one km. (two-thirds of a mile) from city center. Restaurant, dancing. Sauna, tennis, indoor pool; golf nearby. AE, DC, MC, V.

CAMPING

There are 125 camping sites in this area. Some are: **Hörby,** Ringsjöstrand (0415–105 67). 7 cabins. At Lake Ringsjön. Open all year; **Kalmar,** *Stensö Camping,* two km. (1.2 miles) south of Kalmar (0480–207 33). 15 cabins. Camping site open June through Aug.; **Kosta,** *Kosta Camping,* 500 meters (550 yards) southeast of Kosta Glassworks (0478–505 17). 4 cabins; **Kristianstad,** *Charlottsborgs Camping,* three km. (1.8 miles) west of town center (044–11 07 67). 9 beds. **Urshult,** *Urshults Camping,* Rävabacken (0477–202 43). At Lake Åsnen, two km. (1.2 miles) north of Urshult. 9 cabins. Open June through Aug.

HOW TO GET AROUND. By car. If you are driving from Stockholm and Helsingborg is your goal, follow Highway E4 all the way (584 km. or 363 miles). From there, Highway E6 leads into Malmö. A more scenic route to Malmö from Stockholm follows Highway E4 to Norrköping, then swings off on the mainly coastal Highway 15.

By bus and train. From Stockholm, Malmö is seven hours by train, and 10¼ hours by bus. Helsingborg is seven hours by train and nine hours by bus. There are bus services on all major roads. The express bus from Malmö to Kalmar along scenic Highway E66 takes seven hours. There is a bus service from Copenhagen International Airport to Malmö Central Station, crossing on the Dragør–Limhamn ferry, which operates almost hourly throughout the day. There is also an inter-city bus service (Line 999) which operates at frequent intervals from Copenhagen's main railway station via the Dragør–Limhamn ferry to Malmö and Lund.

By air. Malmö is only 25 minutes by air from Copenhagen, but the city's Sturup Airport is inconveniently located almost 20 miles from downtown, so most air passengers now use the frequent hovercraft service run by SAS Scandinavian Airlines. You check in at Copenhagen International Airport in the normal way and the hovercraft runs from a ramp on the perimeter of the airport across the Öresund channel into Malmö harbor, where SAS has built its own terminal.

By Boat. Southern Sweden is linked with Denmark by boat via: Malmö to Copenhagen (1½ hours), Limhamn to Dragör (55 minutes), Landskrona to Tuborg (1½ hours), Helsingborg to Helsingør (25 minutes), Varberg to Grenå (4 hours), Helsingborg to Grenå (3½ hours) and Gothenburg to Frederikshavn (3¼ hours). Traffic is heavy on all runs and the ferries carry cars and, in some cases, international trains. A hydrofoil operates between Malmö and Copenhagen, with regular trips taking only 45 minutes.

TOURS. There are daily sightseeing tours by bus leaving from Gustav Adolfs Torg in Malmö at 11 A.M. and 1 P.M. From June to Aug. Sightseeing by boat through the canals and in the harbor can be enjoyed daily from May through Aug. Tours leave from the quay opposite the Central Station in Malmö every hour between 10 A.M. and 5 P.M.

From May through Aug. there are a number of day tours to the castles, manor houses and churches in Skåne. Call at the Malmö tourist office for details.

PLACES TO VISIT. Apart from the castles, chateaux and manor houses of Skåne and Sweden's "Chateau Country," there are many other attractions in this region. When visiting Malmö, remember the **Malmö card,** which offers free bus transport, free admission to the museums and discounts on restaurants, sightseeing, souvenirs etc. It costs about SEK 65 for three days and SEK 95 for a week. Children half price.

Bosjökloster. 45 km. (28 miles) from Malmö on Lake Ringsjön. Founded in 1080 as Benedictine convent. Garden, exhibitions. Open May to Oct., daily 9–5.30 (0413–250 48).

HELSINGBORG. Fredriksdals OpenAir Museum and Botanical Garden— 18th-century mansion and farmhouses and buildings from Skåne province. Open May through Sept., 10–6.

Kärnan tower (Medieval Keep). View from the ramparts of city and Danish coast. Open May through Aug., daily 9–8.

Rådhuset (Town Hall). Including tourist office.

Slottshagen (Castle Park). Beautiful park within the ramparts. Also the Tosengården with thousands of roses and a fine view of the strait.

Sofiero. A former royal summer residence. Five km. (three miles) north of Helsingborg. Beautiful garden. View of the straits. Open May through Aug., 10–6.

HÖÖR. Frostavallen, 60 km (37 miles) from Malmö or Helsingborg, is a recreation center, hotel, youth hostel, park and zoo with Nordic animals. Also a Stone-Age village where you can stay overnight. Hides and skins are for rent, and you prepare your own Stone-Age meals. Experience how people lived 8,000 years ago. Open all year round (0413-220 60).

KALMAR. Kalmar Castle. Chapel and museum. Museum has archeological finds, weapons, furniture etc. and exhibits from the warship *Kronan.* Open Mar. through Sept., Mon. to Sat. 10–4, Sun. 1–4; Dec. through Feb., Sun. only; rest of year, daily 1–5.

KARLSKRONA. Varvsmuseet (Marine Museum). Amiralitetsslätten. Galleon figureheads, ship models. 300 years of marine history. Open daily 12–4, (July, 12–8).

KRISTIANSTAD. Bäckaskog Castle. 10 km. (six miles) east of Kristianstad. Swedish King Charles XV's summer residence. Chapel, gardens. Open May 15 to Aug., 10–4.

Film Museum. Östra Storgatan 53. Old films (shown on request) and film equipment. Open Tues. to Fri. and Sun. 1–4; closed Mon. and Sat. Admission free.

LANDSKRONA. Ängelholm House. Stora Norregatan 80. Built 1628, the oldest building in Landskrona.

Borstahusen. A genuine village with small houses and alleyways.

Landskrona Museum. At Slottsgatan. European and Swedish art, workshops and shops. Also prehistoric section where you can try out primitive tools. Open daily 1–5. Admission free.

Weilbullsholms flower nurseries. At southern entry to city. Open daily for inspection.

The island of Ven. Half-hour boat trip—flowers, foundations of a castle and a reconstructed observatory called **Stjärneborg** (Star Castle).

LUND. Kulturen Museet (Museum of Cultural History). Tegnérsplatsen. Openair museum with 30 buildings from South Sweden. Exhibits of ceramics, glass, textiles, silver, weapons and toys. Open daily 12–6.

MALMÖ. Malmö Museum. Malmöhusvägen in the **Malmöhus Castle,** dating from 1542. Museum shows art, natural history, history of Malmö. Outside the castle is the **Kommendanthuset,** the Technical and Marine Museums. Open Tues. to Sun. 12–4; Thurs. 5–9; closed Mon., except June through Aug.

ÖLAND. Eketorp—reconstructed fortified village with small museum. 45 km. (28 miles) south of Öland Bridge near Gräsgård. Open May through Sept.; June 6 to Aug. 16, 9–6, otherwise 9–5. Guided tours; call 0485-620 23 for current times. Regular buses from Färjestaden.

VÄXJÖ. Smålands Museum, behind railway station. Large collection of glass and tools, weapons, coins, 18th- and 19th-century art. Open Mon. to Fri. 9–4, Sat. 11–3, Sun 1–5.

Utvandrarnas Hus (the Emigrant Institute). Adjoining the museum (0470-201 20). Archives (research by appointment only). Permanent exhibition of "Dream of America"—the emigration of more than one million Swedes to the New World. Minnesota Day celebrated here each year on the second Sunday in Aug.

Tours of Lake Helaa, on the small steamer *Thor* (built 1887), depart from Kronoberg Castle. Call the tourist office for timetable.

 SPORTS. There are fine sandy beaches at Falsterbo, Mölle, Tylösand, Ängelholm, Malen, Mellbystrand Skrea, Ystad, Åhus, and on the isle of Öland. Most resort hotels have **tennis** courts, and **golf** may be played at several places. 18-hole courses at Båstad, Falsterbo, Kalmar, Landskrona, Lund and Mölle.

Good salmon **fishing** in the Mörrum River, with the season from April-May until September 30. It is advisable to order fishing cards in advance if you come during April or May. Write Hotel Walhalla, Mörrum. Sea-fishing tours are arranged from Helsingborg.

There's a good **horseracing** track near Malmö, at Jägersro, where the Swedish Derby, usually about mid July, draws a big, international crowd.

There are many **biking** and **hiking** trails in the region.

GOTHENBURG AND THE WEST COAST

Gateway to Northern Europe

It is only proper to approach Gothenburg (or Göteborg) from the sea, for at heart it is a product of the oceans and the ships that sail them. Shipping, shipbuilding and fishing set their stamp on this region long before the age of the Vikings. You never get far from the maritime influence, and the harbor bustles (as does the city's ultra-modern airport, Landvetter).

A classic example of honesty, modesty and frankness once was found in a shipping company's guide to Gothenburg. "Gothenburg is by no means a Tourist Mecca," it read, "but it has its points." This is to certify that it does have its points, and plenty of them. Actually, Gothenburg is a gateway to the entire world, with regular freight services and frequent passenger connections to all the Seven Seas. If you come to Scandinavia with one of the Danish or Swedish lines—DFDS Seaways from England or with Stena Line from Germany or Denmark— Gothenburg is your first Scandinavian port of call. And the city is the ideal place to begin a round trip tour of Scandinavia, since it occupies almost the exact center of a triangle of which the capitals of Stockholm, Oslo, and Copenhagen are the points.

Exploring Gothenburg

An intangible air, perceptible enough almost to be held in your hands, distinguishes Gothenburg from Stockholm. Many attribute it to centuries of close relations with Great Britain, birthplace of the Anglo-Saxon tradition of freedom. It has even been called "Little London." The residents are fully conscious of this pronounced attraction westward. Others attribute it to the physical nature of the city, with its broad avenues, its huge, sprawling harbor, its comparatively great geographical area for a city of some 430,000 people. Finally, age has something to do with this sensation. Gothenburg is young, officially born in 1621, when parts of Stockholm's Old Town looked about as they do now. There is something of a friendly rivalry between the cities.

A great Swedish king, Gustavus Adolphus, the "Lion of the North," gave Gothenburg its charter in 1621. He called in Dutch builders, and the canals and architecture will show the strength of their influence. The town soon began to play a part in history. Karl X summoned the parliament to meet there in 1659–60, in Kronhuset, the oldest building extant, and there his son was crowned Karl XI after Karl X's death. Scotsmen and Germans had by this time settled in the town in considerable numbers.

As early as 1699 the British community formed an association for mutual support. The influx of Scots and Englishmen continued through the 18th and 19th centuries, and they and their descendants have had a decisive importance in the commercial and cultural development of the city. Many of the finest old families of Gothenburg have typically English or Scottish names.

At one time Gothenburg enjoyed a thriving trade with the East Indies, as evidenced by the old factory building in the Norra Hamngatan, which now houses the Ethnographical, Archeological, and Historical museums. However, the city's first great commercial impetus resulted from Napoleon's continental blockade in 1806, when its port became the principal depot of British trade with northern Europe.

The opening of the Trollhätte Canal shortly after 1800, connecting Gothenburg by water with huge Lake Vänern and the rich forest and iron products of the region around the lake, offered a new commercial stimulus. Before the middle of the century the first shipbuilding yard was turning out sailing vessels, and industrialization was under way. Today Gothenburg is the headquarters of many industries, including the world-wide SKF ballbearing empire; AB Volvo, Scandinavia's largest maker of automobiles; hyper-modern shipyards; and the Hasselblad camera factory. About one third of the population gets its living from industry. Incidentally, Gothenburg is one of the few remaining cities with streetcars.

Landvetter Airport provides West Sweden with access to very large aircraft with direct links to other countries. This new airport has a capacity that will meet the requirements of the regions for many years. With its location close to Highway 40, the new airport is easy to reach from all the towns in West Sweden. Signposts marked with the airport symbol clearly show the way from the roads in the vicinity.

City Highlights

You must really see the harbor to appreciate it. There are 22 kilometers (14 miles) of quays, 200 cranes that sometimes seem to rise up like steel forests, and the warehouse and customs sheds cover more than 1½ million square feet. Gothenburg is the home port of 40 per cent of the Swedish merchant fleet—better than 4 million tons of shipping—and handles a third of the country's imports and a quarter of the exports. During the summer there are boat tours that take you around the harbor and entrance, as well as through the city's network of canals.

Skandiahamnen is the new port for container and roll-on/roll-off traffic. Here you find the terminals of DFDS Seaways, Atlantic Container Line and other shipping companies.

Gothenburg's Fish Harbor, one of the largest in Scandinavia, opened in 1910. Its early morning fish auction, at which wholesalers publicly bid for cod, catfish, sole, herring, and occasionally even whale, has become something of a tourist attraction.

Trädgårdsföreningen, site of the magnificent gardens of the horticultural society, begins right across the square from the Central Station. The Palm House, erected in 1878 and completely restored recently, is an impressive example of what you can grow in a northern climate with the help of heat and glass.

Götaplatsen is an impressive square which might be described as the cultural heart of Gothenburg. In the center is the famed "Poseidon" fountain by Milles. The columned building which rises up above the broad steps at the end of the square—and dominates it—is the Art Gallery. As you face the art museum, the building on the left is the modern City Theater, the one on the right the Concert Hall. If you climb the steps leading up to the museum, you get a fine view of the wide boulevard Kungsportsavenyen, with the profile of downtown Gothenburg in the distance. This square is notable as an expression of modern architecture, as impressive as older and better-known counterparts elsewhere in Europe.

Liseberg Amusement Park, Sweden's most popular visitor attraction, is only a few minutes from downtown by streetcar or taxi, a walk of only 15 minutes or so from the Park Avenue Hotel. This is one of the best, neatest, and best-run amusement parks in existence—partly because of beautiful gardens that you don't ordinarily find in this kind of establishment. There are several restaurants, open-air concerts, variety theater, and wide range of the usual carnival attractions.

Among other sights are the Sailor's Tower, near the Maritime Museum, a tall monument to seamen who lost their lives in World War I, from which you have an excellent view of the harbor and city; Masthugget Church, a striking modern edifice on an impressive site; Guldheden, a housing development with a pleasant central square; and the huge natural park, Slottsskogen.

There are several good museums with fine, often unique, collections. Anyone interested in shipping should by all means see the Maritime Museum between Karl Johansgatan and route E3.

Gothenburg Environs

In the neighboring industrial town of Mölndal, only a short distance away, is the delightful 18th-century mansion of Gunnebo. It is a good example of architecture and landscaping of a period that combined the best of French and English influence. The house was designed by C. W. Carlberg, who also designed the furniture in 1796. John Hall, a merchant of British origin, was the first owner of Gunnebo. It is now the property of Mölndal community. During the summer visitors are shown around in the early afternoon; there are hourly buses to Mölndal and Gunnebo from Nils Ericsonsplatsen (behind the Central Station).

Särö, a bit farther south, by bus, is known for its thriving foliage and oak trees, which grow right at the edge of the sea. On the route to Särö is the beautifully situated Hovås golf course.

To the east of Gothenburg is a large, hilly forest-and-lake area. Visit the 19th-century Nääs manor house on route E3 (32 kilometers or 20 miles from Gothenburg; hourly tours in the summer). In the outbuildings there are stables, restaurant, coffee shop and several exhibition shops selling traditional Swedish products—textiles, wood, furniture, antiques and souvenirs.

Nearby is the medieval Öijared chapel, in the middle of a 45-hole golf course. Further northeast is the Anten-Gräfsnäs Veteran Railway.

The West Coast

The coast north of Gothenburg (Bohuslän province) is the beginning of fjord country, with its dozens of fishing villages and thousands of islands. Forty minutes from Gothenburg by car lies the former fishing village of Stenungsund, today Sweden's busy petrochemical center. Just outside, the mighty Tjörn bridges span the fjord—the breathtaking view will give you a strong incentive to explore.

North and slightly west of Gothenburg stretches the province of Bohuslän, a coastal and island summer playground among the most popular in Sweden—a part of the famed west coast. It was more or less discovered by the royal family. Prince Vilhelm, brother of the late king, wrote with much great feeling about Bohuslän, beginning with a visit there in the '90s with his father, King Gustav V. "So the ocean, the ships, and the rocky islands form the trinity that characterizes Bohuslän," Vilhelm writes. "A name that sounds good to all seafaring folk, for it bespeaks a coast peopled by strong men and sturdy objects, an archipelago formed of gneiss and granite and water which eternally stretches foamy arms after life."

How to Explore the Area

Proceeding north from Gothenburg, you come to Kungälv, which was a commercial center before the year 1000. It is overlooked by a hugh medieval stronghold, Bohus Fortress, built by the Norwegians in 1308. Kungälv is a sea of flowers during apple blossom time.

The island city of Marstrand was also built by the Norwegians, some time during the 13th century. This was the favorite west coast summer resort of King Oskar II, who died in 1907, and the resort hotel emits something of a turn-of-the-century air. It is still a popular summer resort. There is an interesting 17th-century fortress overlooking the city—Karlsten—used as a prison during the 18th and 19th centuries. The church is from the 14th century.

Lysekil is a popular and reasonably typical example of the villages along the west coast which have become Meccas for summer vacationers. It rests on the mouth of a long fjord, protected from sea and wind by cliffs.

On the other side of the fjord is Fiskebäckskil, another popular summering place. Farther inland, roughly northeast, is the city of Uddevalla, the biggest municipality in this region (population, over 46,000). Uddevalla as a city leaves much to be desired in its appeal to the eye, but is a good overnight halt. The principal industries are textiles, paper, wood processing, and shipbuilding.

Along the coast north of Lysekil are a whole row of villages familiar to west coast vacationers and to the painters and sailors who haunt this region in the summer time—Smögen (a singularly picturesque fishing village), Bovallstrand, Fjällbacka, Grebbestad, and many more. At the very north end of the province, just below the border to Norway, is Strömstad, the northern anchor of the Bohuslän vacation region, so to speak. The city has old traditions both as a port and military objective and as a summer resort. In addition, Strömstad offers you interesting excursions. The best from a historical point of view is to Fredriksten Fortress, just over the Norwegian border at Halden, where King Charles XII fell in 1718. This whole region was bitterly contested for centuries in the Scandinavian wars.

Just 45 minutes by boat from Strömstad are the Koster Islands, a holiday paradise for people who like boating, fishing and swimming in a car-free environment.

The west coast area of Sweden actually stretches about 400 kilometers (250 miles) south from the Norwegian border as far as Laholm. Going south from Gothenburg, you reach the town of Kungsbacka, whose square is the site of a colourful market on the first Thursday of every month. Nearby is Fjärås Bräcka, where an ice-age sand ridge divides Lake Lygnern from the sea. From the top there is a splendid view over this coastal area, as well as over the lake, which resembles those of middle or north Sweden. On the slopes are Iron Age and Viking graves. Also to be found in Fjärås are the largest horse-radish plantations in the country!

Only a few minutes away lies the impressive turn-of-the century Tjolöholm Palace, now open to the public from April through November—hourly tours every day during summer and on weekends in spring and fall—and there is also a "stable" cafeteria, a horse carriage museum, and a park. A few kilometers east of Tjolöholm is the tiny, picturesque 18th-century village of Äskhult, now an open-air museum.

Also nearby are Lerkil and Gottskär on the Onsala Peninsula, the scene of plenty of activity in the small-craft harbors. You might be able to spot some seals on skerries nearby.

South again is Varberg, an industrial center, port and holiday resort. It's only five minutes' walk from the city center to the nearest beach here. The old fortress has sections which date from the 13th century and was once the most formidable stronghold in Europe. Today it contains a unique youth hostel and a museum with the world's only known fully dressed medieval body (the Bocksten Man). Daily fishing tours are offered from Varberg with the prospect of catches of dogfish, cod and mackerel. The Getterön Reserve for migratory birds can boast more species than most similar reserves in Sweden.

Further south is the little town of Falkenberg, known for its salmon fishing and popular among vacationers. The outstanding sight is the stately bridge over the Ätran River, which dates from 1756. The Törngren Pottery, dating from 1789, is also worth a visit.

Halmstad is the center of this tourist region; a provincial capital with some 76,000 inhabitants. The town is about 600 years old and the oldest building is the church, a 14th-century Gothic structure. Miniland, near Halmstad, shows Sweden modelled in miniature (scale 1:25).

Other popular resorts nearby are Tylösand, Laxvik and Steninge.

PRACTICAL INFORMATION FOR GOTHENBURG
AND THE WEST COAST

TOURIST INFORMATION. The tourist office in Gothenburg has information about **Gothenburg** and all the attractions on the West Coast as far as the Norwegian border. The address is Basargatan 10 (031–10 07 40). Open daily 9–6 during the summer; Mon. to Sat. only Sept. to Apr. There is also a tourist office in the Nordstan shopping center (031–15 07 05), open year-round Mon. to Fri. 9.30–6, Sat. 9.30–3; closed Sun.

Other regional tourist offices are at: **Falkenberg,** Sandgatan-Holgersgatan (0346–174 10); **Halmstad,** Kajplan (035–10 93 45); **Kungsbacka,** Storgatan 41 (0300–346 19); **Lysekil,** S. Hamngatan 6 (0523–130 50); **Strömstad,** Norra Hamnen (0526–143 64); **Varberg,** Brunnsparken 39 (0340–887 70).

USEFUL ADDRESSES. Gothenburg. *British Consulate,* Nordstan shopping center, Götgatan entrance (031 –11 13 27). *American Consulate General,* Södra Hamngatan 2 (031–10 05 90).

TELEPHONE CODES. We have given telephone codes for all the towns and villages in the hotel and restaurant lists that follow. These codes need only be used when calling from outside the town or village concerned.

HOTELS AND RESTAURANTS. Many new hotels have been built in Gothenburg recently, so there should be plenty of choice. If you are without a room, use the room-booking service at the tourist office. A low-cost hotel package is available daily from mid-June through mid-Aug. at 30 hotels in Gothenburg and at weekends only for the rest of the year, normally for a minimum two nights' stay. Rates per person per night vary from SEK 195 to SEK 335 (double occupancy) and the package includes breakfast and the Gothenburg card (described below under "How To Get Around"). Reduced prices are available for children. The package is bookable through travel agents.

For the rest of the West Coast, accommodations are in general on the modest side. A few towns draw a more or less fashionable trade, but most of the people who come to the region in summer live in cottages or aboard their sailboats. Many resort hotels offer demi-pension rates (breakfast and dinner) and advantageous pension rates for a stay of three days or more.

The West Coast is dotted with camping sites (more than 75)—most are on beaches and all are up to a good standard. Many also have camping cabins or bungalows for rent.

ÅSA. *Motel E6* (I), Åsa, 17 Km. (ten miles) south of Uddevalla (0340–516 66). 20 rooms. Restaurant with homely fare. MC, V.

GOTHENBURG AND THE WEST COAST

FALKENBERG. *Grand* (M), Ågatan 1 (0346–144 50). 54 rooms. Central, 500 meters (546 yards) to railway station. Restaurant, dancing, sauna; three km. (two miles) to outdoor pool. AE, DC, MC, V.

FISKEBÄCKSKIL. Youth Hostel. *Bassholmen,* three km. (two miles) southeast of Fiskebäckskil (0522–117 87). 38 beds. In the archipelago in a nature reserve. Open June 6 to Aug. 17.

GOTHENBURG. *Ekoxen* (L), N. Hamngatan 38 (Nordstan), (031–80 50 80). 80 rooms. Very central. Oyster bar, whirlpool, sauna. AE, DC, MC, V. *SAS Pårk Avenue* (L), Kungsportavenyn 36–38 (031–17 65 20). 320 rooms. One of Sweden's finest. Double rooms have balconies. Restaurants *Belle Avenue* and *Harlequin,* as well as *Lorensberg* with dancing and floor show. Sauna, pool. AE, DC, MC, V. *Sheraton Göteborg* (L), Södra Hamngatan 59–65 (031–10 16 00). 343 rooms. The city's newest international-standard hotel. Central location near railway station. Built round spacious low-rise atrium lobby. Three restaurants, health center with sauna, solarium, swimming pool and gym. Piano-bar, casino and nightclub. AE, DC, MC, V.

Eggers (E), Drottningtorget (031–17 15 70). 82 rooms. Cozy 19th-century building near railway station. AE, DC, MC, V. *Europa* (E), Köpmangatan 38 (Nordstan), (031–80 12 80). 480 rooms. A few steps from central station and airport bus. 116 shops in big center outside door. Restaurants *Newport, Europa Garden* and *Culinaire. Jonny's* piano bar. Private saunas, pool, nightclub. AE, DC, MC. V. *Gothia* (E), Mässansgatan 24 (031–40 93 00). 300 rooms. View of the city. Near Liseberg and fairground. Restaurant, piano bar on the top floor. Sauna on the 18th floor. Exercise center. Airport bus. AE, DC, MC, V. *Opalen* (E), Engelbrektsgatan 73 (031–81 03 00). 237 rooms. Smoke-free rooms. Close to *Scandinavium,* the Swedish Fairground and Liseberg. *Club Opalen* with dancing. Exotic *Tahonga* bar. Sauna. AE, DC, MC, V. *Ramada* (E), Gamla Tingstadsgatan 1 (031–22 24 20). 121 rooms. 5 mins. from city center by car. Pool. AE, DC, MC, V. *Riverton* (E), Stora Badhusgatan 26 (031–10 12 00). 190 rooms. Restaurant, sauna, near Stena Line terminal. AE, DC, MC, V. *Rubinen* (E), Kungsportsavenyn 24 (031–81 08 00). 189 rooms. Central, on an elegant avenue. Restaurant *Librette* and bistro. Cocktail bar and tearoom. AE, DC, MC, V. *Windsor* (E), Kungsportsavenyn 6 (031–17 65 40). 83 rooms. Secluded British atmosphere, best location. Popular cocktail bar, restaurant. SAS office. AE, DC, MC. V. *Victor's* (E), Skeppsbroplatsen 1 (031–17 41 80). 38 rooms. Most exclusive. Restaurant, sauna. AE, DC, MC, V.

Carl Johan (M), Karl Johansgatan 66–70 (031–42 00 20). 153 rooms. Close to ferries to Germany. Restaurant. AE, DC, MC, V. *Lorensberg* (M), Berzeligatan 15 (031–81 06 00). 120 rooms. In the heart of the cultural center. Breakfast only. AE, MC, V. *Novotel* (M), Klippan 1 (031–14 90 00). 150 rooms. Riverside location near the Älvsborg bridge and ferry terminals. Rooms for disabled travelers and allergy sufferers. AE, DC, MC, V. *Poseidon* (M), Storgatan 33 (031–10 05 50). 49 rooms. Small and centrally-located exclusive hotel in a tastefully-renovated 19th century building. AE, DC, MC, V. *Panorama* (M), Eklandagatan 51–53 (031–81 08 80). 341 rooms. Quiet, central location, airport bus nearby. Restaurant, piano bar. Sauna, pool, free parking. AE, DC, MC, V. *Ritz* (M), Burggrevegatan 25 (031–17 52 60). 108 rooms. Central, no restaurant. Run by Salvation Army. AE, DC, MC, V. *Scandinavia* (M), Kustgatan 10 (031–42 70 00). 323 rooms near the Älvsborg bridge with a view of the harbor. Close to the ferry terminal for Germany. Restaurant *Oscar IV,* dancing. Cocktail bar *Langunen,* on poolside. Free garage. AE, DC, MC, V. *Tre Kronor* (Three Crowns) (M), N. Kustbanegatan 15 (031–80 15 00). 172 rooms. Within walking distance of the shops etc. Restaurant, nightclub, sauna, heated garage. AE, DC, MC, V. *Vasa* (M), Viktoriagatan 6 (031–17 36 30). 44 rooms. Central, breakfast only. Buffet, sauna, solarium. AE, DC, MC, V.

ME-Privata Rumspensionat (I), Chalmersgatan 27A (031–20 70 30). 9 rooms, 3 baths. No credit cards. *Kungsport* (I), Karl Gustavsgatan 21 (031–13 52 36). 6 rooms. No credit cards. *Royal* (I), Drottninggatan 67 (031–17 01 00). 80 rooms. Central. The oldest hotel in Gothenburg. Has charm and atmosphere. On shopping street. Breakfast only. AE, MC, V.

86 SWEDEN

Restaurants. *Fiskekrogen* (E), Lilla Torget 1 (031–13 07 30). 30 fish dishes to choose from. Excellent for lunch. AE, DC, MC, V. *Gamle Port* (E), Östra Larmgatan 18 (031–11 07 02). Central. Fine atmosphere. Pub, nightclub. AE, DC, MC, V. *Johanna* (E), Södra Hamngatan 47 (031–11 22 50). One of the best restaurants in Sweden; French and Swedish cuisine. Closed Sun. AE, DC, MC, V. *Libretto* (E), Kungsportsavenyen 24 (031–81 08 00). Gourmet restaurant in Hotel Rubinen. AE, DC, MC, V.

Bräutigams (M), Östra Hamngatan-Kungsgatan (031–13 60 46). Traditional café. Home-made pastries, sandwiches, salad bar. Also warm dishes. AE, DC, V. *Lai-Wa* (M), Storgatan 11 (031–110239). Open daily. Chinese and Oriental fare. *Räkan* (the Shrimp) (M), Lorensbergsgatan 16, behind Hotel Rubinen (031–16 98 39). Direct your order to your table in small radio-controlled fishing-boats. You can also have your snapps arrive by boat. AE, MC, V. *White Corner* (M), Vasagatan 43 (031–81 28 10). Pub in English style. Steakhouse, cafeteria, music. Open late. AE, DC, MC, V.

Annorlunda (I), Lilla Korsgatan 2 (031–13 80 26). The oldest vegetarian restaurant in Gothenburg. Open until 7 P.M. No credit cards.

In the N.K. department store there are three (M) restaurants: a cafe and lunch restaurant on the fourth floor and *Pub Ferdinand* in the 18th-century vaults. All AE, DC, MC, V.

Liseberg, the amusement park, has many excellent restaurants. You can dine in the open and watch lighted fountains and outdoor performances of various kinds. Some restaurants are open only from April to September. Worth a visit are: *Lisebergs Restaurant* (M), (031–83 62 72). Classical restaurant, dancing. *Wärdshuset* (the Inn) (031–83 62 77). Includes English pub in 18th-century milieu. *Tyrolen* (031–83 62 82). A sing-along place with Tyrolean music every night except Mondays.

Youth Hostels. *Kärralund Camping,* Delsjövägen-Olbersgatan (031–25 27 61). 12 four-bed bungalows. Tram 5. Open all year. *Ostkupan,* Mejerigatan 2 (031–40 10 50). 150 beds. 3 km. (two miles) from city center. Bus 64 from Central Station or tram 5 to St. Sigfridsplan and then bus 62. 30 minutes' walk to Liseberg. SEK 80. Breakfast service, gymnasium, sauna, launderette, T.V. room. Open summer only.

Camping. *Kärralund,* see *Youth Hostels.* Three-star site, open all year round. During the summer months there is a central city camping site at *Valhallabadet.* Two pleasant sites on the coast, both open summer only, are *Askim* (031–28 62 61) and *Lilleby* (031–56 08 67).

HALMSTAD. *Grand* (M), Stationsgatan 44 (035–11 91 40). 120 rooms. Near bus and railway station, close to beaches. Restaurant, sauna. AE, MC, V.

Youth Hostel. At Steninge on the coastal road 18 km. (11 miles) northwest of Halmstad (035–520 54). 49 beds. Open June through Aug.

KUNGSBACKA. *Halland* (M), Storgatan 35 (0300–115 30). 65 rooms. Restaurant *Mistral,* dancing, cocktail bar. AE, MC.

Restaurant. *Leksandsgården* (M), Gottskärsvägen, Onsala (0300–607 05). Ten km. (six miles) from Kungsbacka. Rustic old upper-class milieu. Specialty fish dishes. *Smörgåsbord* Sundays. AE, DC, MC, V.

KUNGÄLV. *Fars Hatt* (M) (0303–109 70). 130 rooms. An inn here since 1684. Restaurant, dancing, sauna, heated outdoor pool. AE, DC, MC, V.

Youth Hostel. Färjevägen 2 (030–189 00). 50 beds. Closed mid-Dec. to mid-Jan. Bus service to Gothenburg.

LYSEKIL. *Fridhem* (I), Turistgatan 13 (0523–141 20). 18 rooms. On the sea, 500 meters (546 yards) from center and bus. Breakfast only. MC, V. *Lysekil* (M), Rosvikstorget 1 (0523–118 60). 50 rooms. Central, seaview. Restaurant, nightclub *Nautic.* Excursions arranged in summer. AE, DC, MC, V.

MARSTRAND. *Alphyddan* (I), Långgatan 6 (0303–610 30). 37 rooms. Close to everything, 50 meters (164 ft.) to outdoor pool. MC.

SMÖGEN. *Havsbadet* (I), (0523–310 35). 25 rooms. 50 meters (164 ft.) from the sea with expansive view. Family-run hotel, restaurant, dancing. Open May through mid-Sept. AE, DC, MC, V.

STRÖMSTAD. *Laholmen* (M), opposite Societetsparken (0526–124 00). 98 rooms. Restaurant, dancing. AE, MC, V.
Youth Hostel. At Norra Kyrkogatan 12 (0526–101 93). 74 beds. Open June to late Aug.

TANUMSHEDE. *Tanums Gestgifveri* (Inn) (M), at bus stop 2.5 km. (1½ miles) east of railway station (0525–290 10). 29 rooms. The inn has been in continuous operation since 1663. Bridal suite with circular bathtub, excellent food. Famous rock carvings nearby. AE, DC, MC, V.

TYLÖSAND. *Tylösand* (E), on the sea eight km. (five miles) from Halmstad (035–30 500). 230 rooms. Restaurant, dancing and nightclub in summer. Sauna, indoor saltwater pool. 200 meters (about 200 yards) to Sweden's most popular golfcourse (36 holes). Open all year. AE, MC, V.

UDDEVALLA. *Bohusgården* (M), on route E6 with panoramic view of the fjord, two km. (1.2 miles) south of Uddevalla (0522–364 20). 115 rooms. Sauna, heated outdoor pool, golf nearby. MC. *Carlia* (M), Norra Drottninggatan 22 (0522–141 40). 66 rooms. Central. Piano bar, dancing. AE, MC, V.
Restaurants. *Gustafsbergs Badrestaurant* (E), five km. (three miles) south of Uddevalla (0522–100 38). In a charming building from the last century. Shrimp evenings Tues. and Thurs. Café on the sea. Dancing May through Aug. 15. AE, DC, MC. V. *Margretelund* (E), Lagerbergsgatan 27 (0522–11830). Turn-of-the-century atmosphere. Fish dish *Hugo Odhén* is a must.

VARBERG. *Statt* (M), Kungsgatan 24 (0340–161 00). 126 rooms. 500 meters (546 yards) to beach. Restaurant, dancing, sauna. AE, MC, V.
Youth Hostel. In the fortress (0340–887 88). 97 beds. Open June through Aug. Spend a night in a guaranteed genuine prison environment. . . .

HOW TO GET AROUND. The Gothenburg card "Göteborgskortet" is your personal key to the attractions of Gothenburg. It gives you free travel on trams and buses, sightseeing by bus and boat, entrance to all museums and the Liseberg amusement park, free trips to Fredrikshavn, Denmark and much more. The price in 1987 was SEK 70 for 24 hours, SEK 105 for 48 hours, SEK 135 for 72 hours and SEK 160 for 96 hours. Cards for children under 15 are cheaper at SEK 40 for 24 hours, SEK 65 for 48 hours, SEK 80 for 72 hours and SEK 100 for 96 hours. The card is obtainable at tourist offices, camping sites, Pressbyrån newspaper kiosks or on board Stena and DFDS ferries.
The minimum fare on a tram or bus is SEK 8. Discount coupons are available. A guided tour by bus will cost you SEK 40 for 50 minutes and SEK 65 for a longer trip.

TOURS. Regular 55-minute sightseeing tours by bus which depart from the Tourist Office at Basargatan 10 (031–10 07 40) give you a good introduction to the city. Don't miss a trip on one of the famous flat-bottomed "Paddan" sightseeing boats which depart from a quay opposite the Tourist Office on a 55-minute tour through the canals and out into the harbor.
There are many passenger boats going along the coast and from the mainland to the islands. There is also a boat package available which will give you an opportunity to get to know the waterways. The cost is approximately SEK 1,000, including accommodations for seven days. There are many boat excursions from Strömstad to Norway, traveling under the Svinesund bridge.

88   SWEDEN

PLACES TO VISIT. GOTHENBURG. All museums in
Gothenburg are open Tues. to Sat. 12–4, Sun. and holi-
days 11–5, Wed. evenings 6–9 except from May through
September, and are also on Mon. from May through
August. The only exceptions are the Fartygmuseet, open Sat. and Sun. only,
11–5; and the Kronhuset, which is not open on Wed. evenings.

Älvsborgs Fästning (Elfsborg Fortress). Historic fortress dating from 1670.
Regular boat trips from Lilla Bommen and Stenpiren during the summer,
including harbor sightseeing. Cafe in fortress.

Botaniska Trädgården (Botanical Garden). South of Slottsskogen Park.
Rock garden, herbarium, hot houses. Open 9 A.M. to sunset.

Fartygmuseet (Ship Museum). Lilla Bommen. Openair museum. See an old
light-ship, old barges, a canoe hewn from a tree trunk, boats from Viking times
etc. Sat. and Sun. only.

Feskekörka (Fish Church). Rosenlundsgatan. Not a church, in fact, but built
like one. It's a fascinating retail fish market where you can buy some of the
delicacies trawled up by the local fishermen. Closed Mon. Nearby is the fishing
harbor, where there is an auction at 7 A.M. every weekday.

Göteborg Museet (Gothenburg Museum). Norra Hamngatan 12, close to
Gustav Adolfs Square. In this building you can find three museums: the **Ar-
keologiska Museet** (Archeological Museum). Prehistoric finds from the west
coast of Sweden, such as arrow heads, fossils etc. **Etnografiska Museet** (Ethnographical Museum). Pre-Columbian Peruvian textiles, South American Indian
cultural artifacts etc. Also a Lapp section. **Historiska Museet** (the local History
Museum). The development of Gothenburg from the earliest times.

Industri Museet (Industrial Museum). Åvägen 24. Articles produced by
industrial concerns in and around Gothenburg; imaginative concepts of the
future; exhibit of veteran cars. Closed Mon.

Konstmuseet (Art Gallery). Götaplatsen. Excellent collections of Dutch and
Italian masters, French Impressionists, Swedish paintings and sculpture from
18th century to the present. Works of Rembrandt, Rubens and Van Gogh.
Closed Mon.

Kronhuset (Crown House). A block from the Gothenburg Museum. 17th-
century building, cobbled courtyard, shops and cafeteria. A living handicrafts
center. Closed Wed. evening.

Röhsska Museet (Röhss Museum of Arts and Crafts). Vasagatan 37–39, off
the main avenue. Displays of Swedish and other furniture, glass, textiles, pewter
etc. Oriental collection. Temporary exhibitions from around the world. Closed
Mon.

Sjöfartsmuseet (Maritime Museum). Stigbergstorget. Devoted to history of
merchant shipping, fishing and Swedish Navy. Many unique models. In same
building the **Aquarium** shows the aquatic life of Scandinavian coastal waters and
lakes. Also the **Sjömanstornet** (Sailor's Tower), a monument to Swedish seamen
who lost their lives in World War I. From the top you have an excellent view
of the harbor and city. Open summer only.

TANUM. Prehistoric rock carvings. At Vitlycke, 1.5 km (about a mile) from
Tanum Church on E6. Guided tours three or four times daily, May through
Aug. Call the tourist bureau (0525-290 60) for exact times.

VARBERG. Museum at Varberg Castle. Provincial farm culture, textiles,
furniture etc. The medieval Bocksten Man, with authentic clothing from that
time. Open June 15 to Aug. 15, daily 10–7; rest of year, Mon. to Fri. 10–4, Sat.
and Sun. 12–4.

Samfärdselmuseet (Museum of Communications). Also at the castle. A small
museum with old wagons, carts, boats and bicycles. Open June 15 to Aug. 15,
daily 10–7.

Varberg Castle. Guided tours every hour on the hour June 15 to Aug. 15,
daily 10–5. Meet the guide at Mellersta Valvet. A small fee.

GOTHENBURG PARKS. Liseberg Amusement Park, only a few minutes from downtown Gothenburg, with beautiful gardens, several restaurants, variety theater and more, is Sweden's most popular tourist attraction.

Slottsskogen, near the Botanical Garden, is a nature reserve with a small zoo and space observatory. Huge park, cafeteria and restaurant. Open daily.

Trädgårdsföreningen, across the square from the Central Station, has acres of magnificent gardens and lawns. See the recently restored Palm House. Outdoor entertainments every week. Restaurant and nightclub.

 SPORTS. Swimming. There are more than a dozen swimming spots around Gothenburg and in the environs of Mölndal, Kungälv and Marstrand. Valhallabadet has an indoor pool in summer, also an outdoor pool.

Golf. 18 holes—at the Gothenburg Golf Club links. Hovås, 15 minutes by bus from Linnéplatsen; also at Delsjön, Albatross and at Öijared, with two 18-hole and one 9-hole courses. Four other courses within 30 minutes by car.

Horseracing and trotting. At Åby, Mölndal, 15 minutes by tram 4.

Football, speedway, skating. At Ullevi, one of the most modern sports stadiums in the world, holding 52,000 spectators.

Athletics. At legendary Slottsskogsvallen, where the Scandinavium stadium, the largest indoor arena in Scandinavia, is located. It can seat 14,000 people. Both Ullevi and Scandinavium are in the center of the city, within walking distance of all hotels.

LAND OF LAKES AND FOLKLORE

Home of the Goths

To the north and east of Gothenburg spreads a broad region known as Sweden's lake district, containing thousands of small lakes, medium-sized lakes, and two of the largest lakes in Europe, Vättern and Vänern. The Göta Canal, a blue ribbon stretching across Sweden, combines some of them with rivers and with manmade channels and locks to create a water route from Gothenburg to Stockholm.

This part of the world, ancient home of the Goths, has been settled for some 4,000 years or more, and has a number of historic sights setting exclamation points to its variegated natural beauty. Each of the region's provinces has its own history and traditions and its own distinct character. The lake district is the cradle of Swedish culture and it is here that most Swedes live.

Västergötland

The name of Västergötland means, literally, "the western land of the Goths"—as contrasted with Östergötland, or the eastern land of the same people. The Swedish Goths apparently originated on the continent of Europe. They were thus at least distant cousins of the barbarians who overran the Roman Empire and made the name Goth a synonym for "one who is rude or uncivilized." Some investigators think this region of Sweden was the first home of the Goths. Others believe that Östergötland should have the dubious honor of having spawned all branches of this people. Certain it is, however, that Västergötland was one of the first regions of Sweden to be settled in the wake of retreating glacial ice. Giant sepulchers have been uncovered from the late Stone Age, about 2500 to 2000 B.C., and so-called gallery graves from the age following.

Geographically, the province is rich in coastline, although it can boast only the small but important piece of the ocean which includes Gothenburg. In the northwest it has some 145 kilometers (90 miles) of the shore of Lake Vänern, the largest fresh-water sea in Western Europe, and to the southeast it has Lake Vättern, not so wide but almost as long. The scenery varies from wooded mountains with rare flora, to the fertile plain around the city of Skara.

Lidköping is a city of some 35,000 people at the inner end of a bay of Lake Vänern, on the southeast shore. It is the oldest city on the lake (its charter was granted in 1446), and is proud of the Rörstrand Porcelain works where 18th-century faience and modern ceramics are made side by side. The principal sight in the city proper is the Old Courthouse, once the hunting lodge of Magnus Gabriel de la Gardie, a powerful politician, noble, and controversial figure from the time of Queen Christina, King Karl X, and his son and successor, Karl XI.

De la Gardie was responsible for an even more impressive structure, however—Läckö Castle. It lies about 24 kilometers (15 miles) north of Lidköping on a beautiful road leading to the end of Kålland peninsula. Actually, the oldest parts of the structure date from 1298, when the building was begun as the residence of the bishop of Skara. De la Gardie—during his brief period of power in the 17th century—made it largely what it is today. Few of the 200-plus rooms are now furnished, but don't miss the chapel, the Hall of Knights, and the guest room prepared for King Karl XI. By one of the ironies of history, it was this king who deprived De la Gardie not only of the Läckö earldom but of most of his other holdings, in a great program of reform reducing the property and power of the nobility. Every summer an exhibition is put on at the castle, which is always worth seeing.

Across the bay to the east from Läckö Castle you see the bold outlines of Kinnekulle, one of the unique "table mountains" of this region. To reach it you will have to retrace your route to Lidköping and move up to Kinnekulle on the eastern side of the bay. Kinnekulle (sounds approximately like "chin-eh-culeh") is notable for two things —the view from its top and the millions of years of geological history it lays open to the naked eye. The process was a complicated one—in brief, Kinnekulle and the other table mountains are masses of subsurface igneous rock which forced themselves up through fissures in the sedimentary rock when this country was still one big sea. When the sea went out and time went to work, the less resistant sedimentary rock was eaten away, but the more durable igneous rock—battered and weather-beaten though it be—still stands. You can study the various layers and get an idea of the whole process at Kinnekulle, besides enjoying the far-flung view.

Moving south and west from Lidköping, you find yourself, after about 24 kilometers (15 miles) of travel through charming country, in the city of Skara, one of the oldest in the country. It was ravaged by war and burned several times, and the only surviving building of any real age is the cathedral. It was founded about the middle of the 11th century, and is probably the second oldest church in Sweden (oldest—Lund Cathedral). Successive reconstructions and additions have mixed the styles—it was originally Romanesque, changed into Gothic, and its exterior is now largely a product of the last century, in traditional high Gothic style.

Skara became a religious center early in medieval times, and has been an educational center since 1641, when one of the first higher institutions of learning in Sweden was established here. Its history goes back to at least 829. If you are a bird watcher, come early in April to see the migrating cranes perform their mating dance at Hornborgasjön. Also near Skara is a newly built "sommarland" or playland for children and the young-at-heart.

Don't miss Varnhem Abbey Church, 16 kilometers (ten miles) or so east of Skara, perhaps the best preserved monastic building in Sweden. It is, furthermore, the outstanding example of the Cistercian Order's considerable building activities in Sweden (well before the Reformation, of course). The Varnhem Abbey Church, started about 1250, is notable—aside from its age and architecture—as the burial place of four medieval kings, Magnus Gabriel de la Gardie (builder of Läckö Castle), and Birger Jarl, founder of Stockholm.

Östergötland and Lake Vättern

The land of eastern Goths, or Östergötland, is a country between two coasts, as different as an imaginative nature could make them. The western coast is formed by Lake Vättern, a long, narrow inland sea around which nestle some of the nation's most treasured natural and historical sights. The east coast is on the Baltic Sea, comparatively harsh and unyielding, but just as beautiful in a bolder fashion. Between are some of the most fertile farmlands and finest estates in the entire country. Linköping, an ancient religious, administrative, and cultural center, lies in almost the exact middle of this luxuriant plain. Norrköping, sometimes inaccurately called a twin city of Linköping, is a modern industrial center forming the northeast anchor of the province on the Baltic Coast.

This whole area can be divided roughly into two regions for purposes of a visit, the east coast of Lake Vättern, ranging from Jönköping, at the southern tip, north as far as the medieval city of Vadstena, and the Linköping-Norrköping area.

Lake Vättern is the second largest lake in Sweden, and its surface area of about 1,000 square kilomteres (750 square miles) ranks it among the major inland seas in Europe. It stretches almost due north and south for nearly a hundred miles, but its greatest width is less than 40 kilometers (25 miles). Around its shores, particularly on the eastern side, lived an ancient culture.

If you approach Lake Vättern from Gothenburg or from the south, your starting point will be Jönköping, at the very southernmost tip of the lake. Jönköping's greatest claim to fame is perhaps as the central stronghold of the Swedish Match Company, a great international enterprise. It was here, about 100 years ago, that the history of one of our most commonplace daily necessities, the safety match, began to be written. The Swedish Match Company still operates a factory and makes its headquarters in Jönköping. There is a museum in the old factory illustrating the history of manufacturing safety matches.

Jönköping is an important administrative center—besides serving as the residence of the provincial governor, it is the seat of the Göta Court of Appeals for southern Sweden. This is the second oldest appeals court in Sweden, and you can see its distinguished building, from about 1650, on the main square. Several of the other buildings, including nearby Christina Church, are from roughly the same period.

Proceeding now along the lake shore, first east and then north, the first main town is Huskvarna, only 6.4 kilometers (four miles) away. It is comparatively young and owes its existence principally to an arms factory moved there shortly before 1700. The factory is still turning out weapons—in newer quarters, of course—and there are other ultramodern plants turning out sewing machines, sporting rifles, chain saws, moped motors, refrigerators and deep-freezers. Specially trained guides show visitors round the factory.

Gränna and Historic Visingsö Island

The next main point of interest is Gränna and, if you are spending any time in this region, you might make this your headquarters. Stay at the Gyllene Uttern (Golden Otter) Inn, situated about 61 meters (200 feet) above Vättern, with a magnificent view of the lake and surroundings (including the isle of Visingsö).

Gränna is never more beautiful than when the fruit trees blossom. You'll see signs along the road advertising *Polkagrisar*— meaning literally "polka pigs"—a kind of red and white striped peppermint candy for which Gränna is famous in Sweden. Do try them, fresh from the hands of the maker.

This little community is the birthplace of a famous polar explorer, and there are two museums devoted to his memory near the site of the house where he was born. His name was S. A. André—and he tried to reach the North Pole by air in 1897. He and two companions started by balloon from an island near Spitsbergen, and disappeared silently into history. More than three decades later the remains of the ill-fated expedition were discovered on White Island, not far from Spitsbergen, and so well-preserved that not only could the diaries be read but the films could be developed.

André was buried in Stockholm with great honors, but the record of his premature tragic death in the cause of science is to be found in the interesting exhibits of the André and Vitö museums in Gränna. See also the ruins of the castle built by Count Per M. Brahe some 300 years ago on road E4. The view is magnificent.

As you look out upon Lake Vättern from Gränna you see a long, narrow island resting peacefully 6.4 kilometers (four miles) across the water. This island, Visingsö, played a role in history up to about 1725. Today there are about a thousand inhabitants, mostly farmers. There is a regular boat service (several crossings a day) to the island from Gränna, and you can easily arrange transportation on the island to see the sights. Join one of the horse-drawn vehicles, which take ten passengers each. The principal sight is the ruined Visingsborg Castle, built around 1550, and last used as a prison for captives taken in Charles XII's wars with Russia, before it burned shortly after 1700. See also the Brahe Church, the 12th-century Kumlaby Church (with interesting murals), the remains of the tower and walls of the medieval castle on the southern extremity of the island. It won't take you long to get around, the whole island is only about 16 kilometers (ten miles) long.

Proceeding north again from Gränna to Vadstena, you come first to Omberg, a national park containing Mount Omberg. There are interesting caves near the shore, but the principal attraction is the broad view from the crown of Mount Omberg, "eight cities, 30 churches, and four provinces."

Ancient Vadstena

Vadstena, the next stop, has all the natural beauties of this region plus unique historical memories. To a great extent Vadstena is the physical reflection of the long and strange life of St. Birgitta (or Bridget), high-born (shortly after 1300) daughter of the royal Folkunga dynasty, mistress of a great estate and mother of eight children, religious mystic, and founder of the Roman Catholic Birgittine Order for women. Birgitta received her instructions from God in the form of visions, which led to the founding of the order in Vadstena. About 1350 she made the strenuous journey to Rome to get the papal blessing and died there in 1373 after a pilgrimage to Jerusalem. Her remains were returned home for burial in the church she designed for Vadstena.

You can easily visit Vadstena on foot. The church is an architectural jewel, begun shortly after 1350 and requiring some 70 years in the building. Aside from the noble Catholic architecture, note particularly the triumphal crucifix, the so-called Lovely Madonna, the Maria triptych at the high altar, the Birgittine triptych showing St. Birgitta presenting her revelations to two cardinals, and—behind the high altar —the lovely coffin containing the recently authenticated relics of the saint and one of her daughters. Also behind the high altar are the confessional stalls once used by the nuns.

Ironically enough, King Gustav Vasa, whose reformation dealt a death-blow to Catholicism in Sweden, chose Vadstena for one of his great fortified castles. The castle is still framed by its protecting moat, but a massive outer wall has disappeared. Construction was begun by King Gustav Vasa about 1540 and the place was used for some time by him and his descendants, but by about 1700 had ceased to be occupied as a royal seat. Note the wedding room (so-called because Gustav Vasa took his 16-year-old bride here about 1550), the small Hall of State, and the chapel.

If you have time, take a look at the interesting old house of Mårten Skinnare (Martin the Tanner) from about 1550, located not far from the church. Theater lovers will be interested in another nearby building, the theater, opened about 1825. It is said to be the oldest provincial theater in the country, and gives you a good idea of what life on the boards was like over a century ago.

Note: Vadstena has acquired quite a reputation within Sweden for its hand-made laces. It will be worth your while at least to have a look at them in one of the shops. Not far from Vadstena are the ruins of the first monastery in Sweden, Alvastra, founded in 1143. Nearby Skänninge is a community at least 1,000 years old, which is mentioned in the text of a 10th-century rune stone. Its Church of Our Lady dates from the late 13th century.

Linköping and Norrköping

Linköping is smaller than Norrköping but vastly more interesting for a pleasure visit. It is an ancient seat of religion and learning, in the middle of a fertile agricultural region. In recent years, a growing industry (most notably aircraft and the SAAB automobile) has forced the idyllic to give ground. Even the cathedral—unhesitatingly called the most beautiful in Sweden by its highly partisan admirers—harmoniously combines both old and new.

You can't miss the cathedral. It is located a block from the central square, where you ought also to study the Milles fountain. (The sculptor Carl Milles was a well-known Swedish-American artist.) The fountain was erected to the memory of the great Folkunga dynasty of the Middle Ages (Birger Jarl, King Magnus Ladulås, St. Birgitta), and shows the progenitor, Folke Filbyter, searching for his lost grandson on a weary horse. Man and beast have traveled together for so long that the sculptor has protrayed them as one living being. The dynasty originated in this area. The oldest part of the cathedral dates from the 12th century, but was really not completed until shortly after 1500, a building period of more than 300 years. The steeple was added only about 75 years ago. Of particular interest are the truimphal crucifix and the baptismal font of the 14th and 15th centuries, the modern altar painting by Henrik Sörensen, and the modern tapestries behind. They are by Märta Afzelius, on a theme from the Creation.

If you have any interest in museums, you ought by all means to see the Provincial and City Museum in Linköping. Examine it as much for the application of modern architectural and display techniques as for the valuable collections.

11 kilometers (seven miles) from Linköping you will find Vreta Cloister, once a thriving establishment of the Cistercian Order. The cloister church, still preserved, was dedicated about 1290 by no less a personage than King Magnus Ladulås himself. The baptismal font of Gotland stone was fashioned before 1300. Several notables, from medieval times on, are buried here. The nunnery itself has fallen into ruins, but you can see fragments of the old walls. The conducted bus excursions from Linköping include both Vreta and some historic manor houses.

Norrköping, fourth largest city in Sweden with 120,000 inhabitants, is notable principally for its industries—largely textiles and wood products. It is one of the major east coast ports. A comparatively young town, the oldest building, Hedvig's Church, is from about 1675. Incidentally Norrköping and Linköping share a full-time professional theater company of high quality, which is particularly remarkable in terms of the relatively small population of the two municipalities. Norrköping is located on a bay of the Baltic Sea, Bråviken, leading out to the archipelago. At the mouth of the bay is Arkösund, a coastal community popular with summer sailors. Kolmårdens Djurpark, 24 kilometers (15 miles) north of Norrköping on Highway E4, is a large zoo, safari park and dolphinarium with camping site, hotel, bathing beach, swimming pool and cableway. There is a regular boat service from Norrköping to the zoo, and the park is open all year round.

Building the Göta Canal

A bountiful Nature in this country of almost 100,000 lakes and rivers provided much of the route ready-made, but man had to do his full share before it was possible to travel between Stockholm and Gothenburg by water. The builders were not interested in tourists—for them the canal was a straight-out commercial freight proposition, of tremendous importance for the country's future. No less than 65 locks were required, as well as kilometers of channels to connect the lakes and rivers. The result was a waterway which tremendously facilitated the movement of freight within and across the country.

In 1800 the Trollhätte Canal connecting huge Lake Vänern with Gothenburg and the North Sea was completed and soon demonstrated its value. Then, in 1808–9, Baltzar von Platen, a military man and ranking government official, advocated the bold plan of continuing on from Lake Vänern to Lake Vättern and across to the Baltic Sea. It is a tribute to the leaders of the country in an era when the whole outlook for the future of the nation was as dismal as it had ever been, that they boldly appropriated 2,400,000 *dalers* to begin the project. It was a tremendous piece of work, and during the years of building ran into constant obstacles and required some five times the original financial appropriation. A masterful piece of hard-headed Swedish logic was applied to overcome one of them. The farmers of one region had refused to sell their land for the right of way. The representative of the canal company asked, "Did you ever see water run uphill?" Nobody could answer in the affirmative. "Well, then," he said, "when this idiot von Platen fails, too, you'll get the land back." The farmers signed. But von Platen *did* make water "run uphill", and it was been doing so in the Göta Canal ever since. Von Platen was never able to take the trip himself: he died shortly before his great dream was realized and the canal opened to traffic. You will find his grave and a statue of him in the city of Motala, on Lake Vättern, one of the cities along the route.

Some of the high points have already been described: Bohus Fortress, Trollhätten Falls, Läckö Castle, Vadstena. You can take it easy, seeing the various sights as thoroughly or superficially as suits you, enjoying the company of your 50-odd fellow passengers. You come in intimate contact with the countryside—here and there the grass alongside the narrow channel and the overhanging trees actually brush the rails and decks. You also see an almost unlimited variety of drawbridges.

You come out on the island-strewn Baltic Sea just south of Norrköping, and follow the coast north for a way before turning into the Södertälje Canal. The canal carries you into Lake Mälar, which brings you, via the beautiful channel from the west, right to the heart of Stockholm. You tie up at Riddarholmen—rested, full of fresh air, and with a real mental image of the heart of Sweden. There are many day tours available on the canal, such as the trip between Söderköping and Arkösund, between Berg and Motala, and on the canal's western leg from Lake Vättern.

Romantic Värmland

Perhaps no other region of Sweden has been so romanticized as the province of Värmland. Sweden's greatest authoress, Selma Lagerlöf, made it a national legend in *The Saga of Gösta Berling,* and there is a widely sung, melancholy, hauntingly beautiful song titled *Song of Värmland.* It is often an anticlimax to visit a region which has been sung in song and story, Värmland will not disappoint you.

Don't be deceived by the endless woods and the idyllic nature of the landscape. The woods, the rivers, and the iron ore of the ground actually make this a leading industrial region, with ultra-modern factories dotted here and there in pleasant, comparatively small towns. The wood and iron ore industries have centuries-old traditions, and the old semi-rural culture was based to some extent on them.

Karlstad is the provincial capital and seat of the diocese, with some 74,000 inhabitants. The oldest building is the cathedral, built between 1723 and 1730. There is a comparatively large harbor on Lake Vänern which has direct connections with the ocean through the Trollhätte Canal.

The origins of Karlstad are lost in antiquity, but because of destructive fires the city hardly looks old. It has apparently been the capital of this region from the beginning of time and was formerly known as Tingvalla, after the *ting,* or meetings of the legislature, which were held here. When Duke Karl issued it a charter in 1584, he also gave it a name. Karlstad means "the city of Karl".

Värmland is cut by rivers and long narrow lakes, running roughly north to south (with a slight bias of the southern end of the axis to the east). The largest of these, and the best known, is the Fryken chain consisting of three lakes. The most popular sightseeing route is the Fryken Valley. You can rent a raft and enjoy a peaceful trip down the Klarälven River.

A tour along the following lines can be managed easily in one day by car. During the summer season, you will find guided bus tours to the principal points of interest. Take the main road north along the beautiful Klarälven River (in the spring full of timber being floated down to factories) about 40 kilometers (25 miles) to Ransäter, where you will find a rural museum, a lookout tower, and the home where Erik Gustaf Geijer, a national literary great, was born in 1783. A few kilometers farther on you come to Munkfors, site of one of the major steel plants of the Uddeholm Corporation. It will give you an idea of the highly-developed quality steel industry of this part of the world. Just north of Munkfors, turn off to the right on the road to Sunnemo. It brings you down to the narrow lake called Lidsjön. The Sunnemo church is a little known exquisite rural parish church, utterly charming in its modest expression in wood of the people's religious feeling. Note the individual carved shingles.

From here you proceed north again along Råda Lake to Uddeholm, a deceivingly peaceful village of 500 souls or so. You'd never know by looking at it, but this is the main headquarters of a huge international corporation. It is truly peaceful. But inside some of the unprepossessing buildings, direct telephone and teletype lines keep Uddeholm in constant touch with its far-flung empire, with its many plants producing iron and steel, wood products, chemicals, and paper, with its sales organization in two hemispheres. The Uddeholm Corporation descends in a direct line from a 17th-century ironworks, and today it is perhaps the largest private employer in Sweden.

Selma Lagerlöf's Home

Now, your best bet is to continue around the north end of the lake, then turn due south again and make your way back to Munkfors. But here, instead of returning directly to Karlstad, you can cut almost due west (to the right) to Sunne, which brings you into the very heart of the Selma Lagerlöf country. It's only 55 kilometers (34 miles) south of here to Mårbacka, her ancestral home, now a public museum maintained largely as she left it at the time of her death in 1940. You are better advised to go back to Sunne from Mårbacka, cross over to the west side of the Fryken Lakes, and turn south towards Karlstad again. Only a couple of kilometers below Sunne you reach famed Rottneros, the "Ekeby" of the Lagerlöf book, a truly fine example of the old culture of the landed gentry, distinguished by sculptures, flowers and a wonderful view. The buildings themselves are stately, and the grounds, overlooking the lake, are well kept. About 16 kilometers (ten miles) before you reach Karlstad, near Kil, is the Apertin Manor House. It's worth a look, but, since it is privately owned, don't expect to get inside without special arrangements. The same thing applies to Rottneros, although the public is permitted to wander freely through the grounds. There is an entrance fee. While in the area, the more adventurous might like to try an elk safari, arranged some evenings by the Sunne tourist bureau.

The city of Filipstad, about 64 kilometers (40 miles) from Karlstad, has a special interest for Americans. It is the home ground of John Ericsson, whose iron-clad ship, the *Monitor,* meant victory at sea for the North in America's War Between the States. Ericsson's place in history would have been assured had he never seen America, however, for he contributed a number of major inventions to the exploding technological progress of the 19th century. Because of his contribution to American national unity, his body was delivered to Sweden in 1890 by the United States Navy, and buried with great pomp. You will find his tomb, and a memorial statue, in this idyllic little city where he grew up. The population is now something over 7,000, and there is a varied industry. The peaceful appearance of the city belies its industrial and commercial importance, however, and it is perhaps never more beautiful than in the spring, when the high waters of the Skiller River go rushing through the heart of the town, almost on a level with the sidewalks.

Dalsland and Its Canal

The province of Dalsland is for lovers of the outdoors. It is shaped in the form of a huge, irregular wedge, with Bohuslän and Norway forming the western border, Lake Vänern the eastern, and the province of Värmland the northern.

Actually, the most beautiful part of Dalsland is perhaps not the coastal regions but the deep forests and lakes of the western and northern areas. The principal tourist centers are Bengtsfors, the northwest anchor of the lovely Dalsland Canal; Ed, on the road to Norway; and Åmål, the principal city.

The Dalsland Canal, built in 1860 under the direction of Nils Ericsson, brother of John Ericsson of U.S. Civil War fame links up a 272-kilometer (169-mile) waterway with no less than 29 locks. You can travel by boat from Köpmannebro on the shores of Lake Vänern up through the whole of northern Dalsland, over the aqueduct at Håverud, and on by the way of Värmland lakes to the Norwegian border.

The Dalsland Canal is actually a system of lakes and only 9.6 kilometers (six miles) is excavated canal. Most indigenous Swedish mammals can be found in this area, including some rare creatures like the lynx and beaver, which have quite large populations here. This is real canoe country and numerous tours are offered, from one to two days up to three weeks. Many tourists also come to see the aqueduct at Håverud and its busy boat traffic. There is an exhibition there showing what the Dalsland region produces and its major sights and attractions.

Dalarna

Sweden's ancient folklore traditions are probably maintained more strongly in the province of Dalarna than in any other part of the country. Every village has its maypole—originally a pagan fertility symbol—which is ornately decorated at midsummer each year and is the focus of the annual festivities marking the longest day. The traditions are strongest in the area round Lake Siljan in the middle of Dalarna. If you visit the area at midsummer you'll see hundreds of villagers, dressed in regional costumes, arriving in their long-boats for a special service in the village church at Rättvik.

Not far from Rättvik is the village of Nusnäs, where the traditional brightly-painted Dalarna wood-carved horses are produced in vast quantities. Nearby is the small but elegant town of Mora, home of the Swedish artist Anders Zorn. A new tourist attraction in the neighborhood is Santaworld (otherwise known as Tomteland), where there are special activities for children year-round. The Grönklitt bear sanctuary near Orsa, where the animals live in a natural forest habitat, is also well worth visiting.

The main town in Dalarna is Falun, where copper has been mined for some 900 years. The best-known landmark is the "Great Pit," a huge hole in the ground which has been there since the mine caved in 300 years ago. You can put on helmet and overalls and go down into some of the old sections of the mine and see the grim conditions under which the miners used to work. It's also well worth visiting the nearby home of the well-known Swedish artist Carl Larsson in an idyllic lakeside location. His simple paintings owe much to the local folk-art tradition.

The "Bergslagen" Region

The name of this region derives from the "bergslag", co-operatives formed by the mining communities holding mineral rights. People first moved to the Örebro and Västmanland counties to work the "öres" in the early middle ages. There are still many traces of blast furnaces, blackened sites of charcoal piles and the homes and other buildings of these early miners. The iron industry is still flourishing in places like Hällefors, Karlskoga and Degerfors.

Strömsholms Castle at Lake Mälaren is a popular tourist attraction with its many horses and stables. Refreshments are served in the kitchen of the castle in summer. The Strömsholms Canal was built to transport the iron and ore of the region. These 96.5 kilometers (60 miles) of waterway and 26 locks are a popular route for smaller craft.

At Engelsberg you can see an old smelting house and relics from the Norberg mining area dating from the 14th century. From the middle of the last century until the 1920s, the power transmission system constructed by the Swedish inventor Christopher Polhem was still in use here. You can see the "Polhem Wheel" measuring 15 meters (49 feet) in diameter, well-preserved after so many years. The 400-year-old silver mine at Sala is also open to the public during the summer months.

Sörmland

South of Lake Mälaren and bordering Stockholm is Södermanland, a province of manor parks and pastoral beauty. You can take the steamer from Stockholm to Mariefred and then join a narrow-gauge veteran railway. In Mariefred is Gripsholm Castle, one of the best-known Swedish historical monuments. Mariefred also houses the national portrait collection—the largest in Europe. Strängnäs and its cathedral is nearby.

Have you ever owned a Swedish pocketknife? If you have, it was manufactured in Eskilstuna. The Rademacher Smithies here are a must to see. There's also a zoo with many rare animals, such as the panda and snow leopard. There are some 50 prehistoric sites near Eskilstuna. The best-known are the Sigurd rock carvings.

Ancient Sweden—One Hour from Stockholm

Sweden begins in Gamla Uppsala (Old Uppsala). It is here that the first Swedish kings, Aun, Egils and Adils, are buried. See the tombs and drink real Viking mead from big horns at the Odinsborg.

The magnificent Gothic cathedral in Old Uppsala is 800 years old and is the seat of the Archbishop of Sweden. Nearby on a hill is the Castle with the Coronation Hall and dungeons—over 400 years old. Carl Linnaeus or Carl von Linné, the world famous botanist and scientist, had his home here, in Hammarby. In the botanical garden in Uppsala there are still living plants dating from the days of Linnaeus. The university at Uppsala, the oldest in Scandinavia, is more than 500 years old.

This was also a mining district. In the 17th and 18th centuries Österby Bruk and Leufsta were the largest ironworks in the country. The Walloons came here to teach the Swedes how to make iron and were the origin of "Swedish" family names like De Laval, Hubinette and Gille. There are many folk festivals and music weeks at Österby Bruk.

PRACTICAL INFORMATION FOR THE LAND OF
LAKES AND FOLKLORE

TOURIST INFORMATION. The most important tourist offices, all open all year round, are at the following places: **Arvika,** Stadsparken (0570–135 60). **Borås,** Torggatan 19 (033–16 70 90). **Eskilstuna,** Fristadstorget 5 (016–10 22 50). **Falun,** Stora Torget (023–836 37). **Karlskoga,** Centralplan 1 (0586–563 48). **Karlstad,** Södra Kyrkogatan 10 (054–19 59 01). **Kolmården Zoo,** summer only (011–950 06). **Lidköping,** Gamla Rådhuset, summer only (0510–835 00). Mariefred, Rådhuset (0159–102 07). **Norrkoping,** Drottninggatan 18 (011–15 15 00). **Örebro,** Drottninggatan 9 (019–13 07 60). **Rättvik,** Torget (0248–109 10). **Sunne,** Mejerigatan 2 (0565–135 30). **Uppsala,** Smedsgränd 7 (018–11 75 00). **Västerås,** Storatorget 5 (021–16 18 30).

TELEPHONE CODES. We have given telephone codes for all the towns and villages in the hotel and restaurant lists that follow. These codes need only be used when calling from outside the town or village concerned.

HOTELS AND RESTAURANTS. Accommodations in this region are modest on the whole. Many of the vacationers who come here stay in cottages and on sailboats.

ALINGSÅS. *Scandic* (M), Bankgatan 1 (0322–140 00). 67 rooms. Has Sweden's only potato-specialty restaurant to commemorate local lad Jonas Alströmer who introduced it to Sweden. AE, DC, MC, V.

ARVIKA. *Bristol* (I), Kyrkogatan 25 (0570–13 280). 40 rooms. Central, with sauna club. Golf, tennis nearby. Breakfast only. AE, DC, MC, V. *Oscar Statt* (M), Torggatan 9 (0570–197 50). 45 rooms, 10 baths. Breakfast only. AE, DC, MC, V.
Restaurant, *Stavnäsgården "Kvarnen"* (The Mill) (M), Klässbol, 15 km. (9 miles) south of Arvika. Cafeteria with home-baked bread. Don't miss the linen weaving mill. Open May to Aug., Mon to Fri. 11–6, Sat. 10–3, Sun. 11–8. AE, MC, V.

BENGTSFORS. *Dalia* (M), Karlbergsvägen 3 (0531–116 50). 45 rooms. 400 meters (440 yards) from Dalsland Canal and near Gammelgården, the homestead museum. Resort hotel, restaurant, cafeteria, sauna, golf, illuminated ski trail, ski lifts. AE, DC, MC, V.

BORÅS. *Grand* (M), Hallbergsgatan 14 (033–10 82 00). 167 rooms. Excellent location in center of town overlooking the river. AE, DC, MC, V. *Hotel Borås* (M), Sandgärdsgatan 25 (033–11 70 20). 53 rooms. Member of the Romantik Hotels group. Exclusive atmosphere. AE, DC, MC, V. *Gustav Adolf* (M), Andra Villagatan 5 (033–10 81 80). 37 rooms. Modern hotel in quiet but central location. AE, DC, MC, V. *Vävaren* (M), Allégatan 21 (033–10 00 20). 80 rooms. A well-run family hotel in the city center. Sauna, cafeteria. Golf and tennis in the outskirts. AE, DC, MC, V.

BORLÄNGE. *Brage* (M), Stationsgatan (0243–241 50). 94 rooms. Restaurant, dancing, piano-bar, sauna. Central. AE, DC, MC, V. *Gylle Värdshus* (Inn) (I), two km. (1.2 miles) from center of Borlänge (0243–119 00). 32 rooms. Cafeteria. AE, DC, MC, V.

ESKILSTUNA. *Country Hotel* (I), Strängnäsvägen (016–11 04 10). 59 rooms. Restaurant, cocktail bar, dancing, sauna. Close to golf, trotting track and ice hockey. AE, DC, MC, V.
Restaurants. *Sommarrestaurangen* (Summer Restaurant) (M), in the zoo (016–14 73 80). No credit cards. *Jernberghska Gården* (I), at the Rademacher forge museum (016–14 65 05). Also outdoor service. Closes 4 P.M. in winter and 6 P.M. in summer.

FALUN. *Grand* (M), Trotzgatan 9 (023–187 00). 183 rooms. Restaurant *Moriska Gården,* cocktail lounge. Sauna, pool. AE, DC, MC, V. *Birgittagården* (I), Uddnäs, Hosjö (023–321 47). 18 rooms.

FILIPSTAD. *Hennickehammars Herrgård* (Manor House) (M) (0590–12 565). 57 rooms. 18th-century manor house by Lake Hemtjärn in a wonderful park. Excellent cuisine—restaurant. Sauna, tennis, fishing, ski sports, rowing boats, canoeing, 15 km. (nine miles) to golf. AE, DC, MC, V.
Restaurants. *LÅngbans Gästgiveri* (inn) (E), John Ericsson homestead (0590–221 69). In an old stable at the mineral-rich LÅngban. Fish and game special-

ties. *Storhöjden* (E) (0590–103 13). In an old house with a view of the city. Outdoor tables. Outlook tower. AE, MC, V.

GRYTHYTTAN. *Grythyttan Gästgivaregård* (Inn) (M), (0591–143 10). 60 rooms. Family-owned inn from 1640. Well-located by old market place. Known for good food and excellent wine cellar. Golf, fishing etc. AE, DC, MC, V.

JÖNKÖPING. *Grand* (M), Hovrättstorget (036–11 96 00). 60 rooms, 33 baths. A fine old hotel, tastefully renovated. A few steps from the shopping area. AE, DC, MC, V. *Ramada* (M), Strandvägen 1 (036–14 24 00). 101 rooms. North of Huskvarna-Jönköping. Most rooms have view of Lake Vättern. Restaurant, cocktail bar. Sauna, pool, golf. AE, DC, MC, V.
  Restaurants. *Svarta Börsen* (E), Kyrkogatan 4 (036–11 22 22). Cosy restaurant in the center of town. New French cuisine. Char from Lake Vättern; crow! AE, DC, MC, V. *Mäster Gudmunds Källare* (M), Kapellgatan 2 (036–11 26 33). Nice atmosphere in cellar vaults. Smörgåsbord. AE, MC, V. *Warpa Skans* (M), on Lake Vättern and the E4 (036–14 21 00). 50 meters (164 ft.) from Brunstorp Inn, north of Huskvarna. *Smörgåsbord,* country-style. Geared for bus groups. AE, MC, V.

KARLSKOGA. *Stadshotellet Alfred Nobel* (I), Torget 1 (0586–364 40). 74 rooms. Nightclub, piano bar. Facilities for handicapped and non-smoking guests. AE, DC, MC, V.

KARLSTAD. *Stadshotellet* (E), Kungsgatan 22 (054–11 52 20). 140 rooms. On the Klarälven River, central, centuries of tradition. Restaurants, cocktail bar, nightclub, sauna, pool. AE, DC, MC, V. *Winn* (M), Norra Strandgatan 9–11 (054–10 22 20). 177 rooms. Modern, centrally located hotel. AE, DC, MC, V. *Gösta Berling* (I), Drottninggatan 1 (054–15 01 90). 75 rooms. Genuine Värmland atmosphere in the center of Karlstad. Restaurant, cocktail bar, sauna. AE, DC, MC, V.
  Restaurants. *Inn Alstern* (E), Morgonvägen 4 (054–13 49 00). Beautifully situated with a view of Lake Alstern. Gourmet food. AE, MC, V. *Skogen-Terrassen* (E), in Mariebergsskogen (054–15 92 03). Nicely situated in one of the leading openair museums and amusement parks in the country. Specializes in food from the area. MC, V.

KOLMÅRDEN. *Vildmarkshotellet* (E), (011–15 71 00). 218 rooms. Fantastic view of Braviken bay. Indoor pool, sauna, nightclub. Near the famous zoo and safari park. MC.
  Youth Hostel. *Kvarsebo* (011–960 46). 32 beds. Coffee, kitchen. Bus to Koln Zoo. Open end June to beginning Aug.

LEKSAND. **Youth Hostel.** *Parkgården,* on route 70, two km. (1.2 miles) south of center (0247–101 86). 84 beds. Sauna, bikes for rent. Bus or train to Tällberg. Open May to mid-Sept.

LIDKÖPING. *Stadshotellet* (M), Gamla Stadenstorg 1 (0510–220 85). 71 rooms. In old town, not far from Lake Vänern. Close to Rörstrand porcelain works and museum. Restaurant. AE, DC, MC, V.

LINKÖPING. *Ekoxen* (E), Klostergatan 68 (013–14 60 70). 118 rooms. Central, beside a park. Restaurant, cocktail bar, sauna, pool. AE, DC, MC, V.
  Restaurants. *Wärdshuset Gamla Linköping* (Old Linköping Inn) (M), Gästgivaregatan 1 (013–13 31 10). In house from 18th century with beautiful painted ceilings. Self-service in genuine cellar vaults. AE, MC. *Restaurang och Cafe Må Gott* (I), Stora Torget (013–11 06 47). In old Lagerström House. Salads and small dishes. Also outside tables. AE, MC, V.
  Youth Hostel. *Centrumgården Ryd* (013–17 64 58). 70 beds. Sauna. Buses to center and railway station. Open June to mid-Aug.

MARIEFRED. *Gripsholms Värdshus* (I), Mariefred (0159–100 40). 10 rooms. Reached by steamer from Stockholm, near the famous 14th-century castle. Claims to be Sweden's oldest hotel, dating from 1623. AE, DC, MC, V.

MORA. *Mora Hotel* (M), Strandgatan 12 (0250–117 50). 92 rooms. On the shores of Lake Siljan and opposite the old church. Sauna, pool. AE, DC, MC, V.
Youth Hostel. *Prästholmens Camping* (0250–163 15). 44 beds. Kitchen, cafeteria, food store and indoor pool on grounds. Open year-round.

NORRKÖPING. *Grand* (E), Tyska Torget 2 (011–19 71 00). 242 rooms. Restaurant, piano bar, wintergarden, sauna. AE, DC, MC, V. *Strand* (I), Drottninggatan 2 (011–16 99 00). 16 rooms. Breakfast only. No credit cards.
Restaurants. *Palace* (M), Gråddgatan 13 (011–18 96 00). Gourmet food, with a view of the river. MC, V. *Palace Café* has chairs outside in summer. Known for plank steak and *Caféflorett* nightclub. Music every night in café. AE, DC, MC, V. *Peter's Steakhouse* (M), Trädgårdsgatan 6B (011–18 31 30). Rustic, paintings, grouped sofas. Closed July; Sun. AE, DC, MC, V.

ÖREBRO. *Grev Rosen* (Count Rosen) (M), Södra Grev Rosengatan 2 (019–13 02 40). 73 rooms. Five minutes' walk from railway station. Cafeteria. Swedish fare at low-price lunch. AE, DC, MC, V.
Restaurants. *Gyllene Drotten* (Golden Ruler) (M), Drottninggatan 15 (019–11 77 82). Central, cellar vaults. AE, MC, V. *Två Krögare* (Two Innkeepers) (M), Rudbecksgatan 18 (019–11 13 67). Central. Good food in pleasant surroundings. AE, MC, V.

ORSA. *Grönklitt Stugby* (M), 79400 Orsa. (0250–46043); bookings 0250–52163.) 12 km. (7 miles) from Orsa. Bungalows; 16 double rooms. Trails, skilifts, saunas, outdoor pool, fishing, minigolf, tennis, shop, restaurant serving local dishes. Adjoins the largest bear park in Europe.

SÖDERKÖPING. *Söderköpings Brunn* (Spa) (M), Skönbergagatan 36 in large wooded park on the Göta Canal (0121–109 00). 110 rooms. Historic spa hotel from 1774. Entertainment in park, dancing, sauna. AE, DC, MC, V.

SUNNE. *Selma Lagerlöf* (M), (0565–130 80). 156 rooms. New hotel built in old Värmland manor-house style. AE, DC, MC, V.

SVARTA. *Svarta Herrgård* (I), (0585–500 03). 41 rooms. Late 18th century manor house in a rambling garden, near Kilsbergen mountain range. AE, DC, MC.

TÄLLBERG. *Green* (M) (0247–502 50). 100 rooms. Timber building, dating from 1917. Wonderful view of Lake Siljan. Some rooms with open fireplaces. Unique art collection. Staff dressed in folk costumes. Restaurant, cocktail bar. Five saunas, golf, tennis, outdoor and indoor pools, dancing on Sat. AE, DC, MC, V. *Åkerblads* (I) (0247–508 00). 64 rooms. Typical Dalarna farmstead dating back to the early 17th century which has been a hotel since 1910 and now run by the 14th and 15th generations of the Åkerblad family. DC, MC, V. *Tällbergsgården* (I), (0247–500 26). 50 rooms. Family atmosphere, fine view of Lake Siljan. Restaurant, cocktail bar, cafeteria. Sauna, golf, tennis, bikes, skis. Smörgåsbord served every day. Folk fiddlers entertain on Sun. AE, DC, MC, V.

UPPSALA. *Linné* (E), Skolgatan 45 (018–10 20 00). 116 rooms. Central. All rooms face the Linné botanical gardens. AE, DC, MC, V.
Restaurants. *Slottskällan* (Castle Spring) (E), Sjukhusvägen 3 (018–11 15 10). In house dating from 18th century, below the castle at the swan pond. AE,

MC, V. *Domtrappkällaren* (M), St. Eriksgränd 15 (018–13 09 55). In the oldest building near the Cathedral (Domkyrkan). Restaurant established 1939. Good Swedish food, also coffee with home-baked bread, ice cream. AE, DC, MC, V.

Youth Hostels. *Sunnersta Herrgard* (Manor House), about six km. (four miles) south of the center (018–32 42 20). 88 beds. Open May through Aug. *Gläntan,* Norbyvägen 46 (018–10 80 60). 50 beds. 1.6 km. (one mile) from the center. Bus 6 or 7 from Stora Torget (the main square). Kitchen, coffee, sauna. Open from end of June to middle of Aug.

VADSTENA. *Vadstena Klosters* (I) (0143–115 30). 25 rooms. *Birgitta Systrarna* (I), Myntbacken 2 (0143–109 43). 22 rooms. Also pension.

Restaurants. *Munkklostret* (the Monastery) (M), (0143–130 00). Medieval atmosphere. Fish from Lake Vättern is specialty. AE, DC, MC, V. *Värdshuset Kungs Starby* (M), near the south entrance to Vadstena from road 50. 75-year-old building, outdoor service in summer, large park. Smörgåsbord every day. AE, DC, MC, V.

Youth Hostel. *Vadstena Vandrarhem,* Skänningegatan 20 (0143–103 02). 65 beds. Walking distance to sights. Tåkern bird sanctuary, eight km. (five miles) away. Bike rental.

VÄSTERÅS. *Park Hotel* (E), Gunnilbogatan 2 (021–11 01 20). 139 rooms. Restaurant, nightclub, dancing, sauna. AE, DC, MC, V. *Stora Hotellet* (M), Vasagatan 15 (021–13 72 90). 80 rooms. A family-owned hotel. Central, walking distance to restaurants, shopping. Sauna. AE, DC, MC, V.

Restaurants. *Bacchus Källare* (M), (021–11 56 40). In a building dating from 17th century. Near the Svartå River. Central. AE, MC, V. *Johannes* (M), Stora Torget (021–13 06 63). Central. Well-known restaurant with excellent food. Outdoor service in summer. AE, DC, MC, V.

Campsites, The following campsites have bungalows or rooms to rent. It is advisable to book a few days in advance: Dals-Långed, Laxsjön (0531–300 10); *Lidköping,* Framnäs (0510–268 04); *Mora,* Mora Camping (0250–265 95); *Norrköping,* Himmelstalund (011–17 11 90); *Rättvik,* Siljansbadet (0248–116 91); *Sunne,* Kolsnäsudden (0565–113 12); *Tärnsjö,* Osta (0292–430 04); *Vadstena,* Vätterviksbadet (0143–127 30).

HOW TO GET AROUND. By car or train. The best way to see a lot of this region is to take the main highway or the train from Gothenburg to Stockholm, or from Stockholm to Karlstad. The section of road between Vadstena and Jönköping is one of the most spectacular, with the road winding along the eastern shore of Lake Vättern.

Karlstad is easily reached by car or train from Gothenburg or Stockholm. If you go from Gothenburg, you will pass the lakes and forest of Dalsland and should plan to stop at Håverud to see the locks of the Dalsland Canal.

Linköping and Norrköping are respectively 217 km. (135 miles) and 145 km. (90 miles) from Stockholm and are close enough for a day excursion. There are daily bus tours to Kolmården Zoo.

By air. The area is well served by air. From Stockholm there are 16 flights a day to Borlänge/Falun, eight to Karlstad, nine to Jönköping, and five to Norrköping.

By boat. You can see this region with graceful ease by boat on the Göta Canal, a waterway which is more than 100 years old. Several boats ply the Göta Canal, offering tours of varying length. There are boats that go from Söderköping to Arkösund, from Norsholm to Söderköping, and from Karlsborg to Töreboda. If you are at Trollhättan, you can take the *Strömkarlen* on a canal tour. For schedules call 0141-100 50 or call at the nearest tourist bureau.

The traditional tour to take on the canal is the three-day trip on the *Diana, Juno* or *Wilhelm Tham.* They operate between the middle of May and the beginning of September. You can book this tour through your travel agency before you leave for Sweden. You can also rent your own boat by phoning *Boatco* (0431–340 93).

Boats also operate on the big lakes such as Fryken in Värmland, the Siljan in Dalarna and the Vänern and Vättern.

By bicycle. There are many bicycle trails in this region and maps for them are available in book shops or at the tourist bureaux. In particular, look for maps of a marked trail called "Mälardalsleden." There is also a biking or hiking trail along the Göta Canal, where oxen once drew barges.

You can rent bicycles in Söderköping (0121-134 75), Borensberg (0141-400 60), Töreboda (0506-104 96), or in Sjötorp (0501-510 03).

 PLACES TO VISIT. In addition to the veritable inland seas of Lakes Vänern and Vättern and the Göta Canal which wends its scenic way from Stockholm to Gothenburg, there are many other distinctive glimpses of past and present in this region.

ESKILSTUNA. Djurgården Museum and Sörmlandsgården. At Carlavägen-Djurgårdsvägen. Openair museum showing local history. Sörmlandsgården is an early 19th-century farm complete with stables, hay barn etc. Open May through Sept., daily 11–4.

Rademacher Smedjorna. The Rademacher Smithies, built in 1658 and now an openair homestead museum. Demonstrations in the copper and iron smithies; a hatter making hats and tin soldiers being made in the tin foundry. Also an industrial and armory museum nearby (closed Mon.). Daily performances at the Rademacher in Jul. Cafeteria. Open daily 10–4; Jul. through Aug., Mon. to Fri. 10–6, Sat. and Sun. 10–4. Admission free.

GRÄNNA. Andrée Museet. Pictures and memorabilia of S.A. Andrée's unsuccessful attempt to reach the North Pole by balloon in 1897. Open May through Aug., daily 12–5; Sept., daily 12–4; closed rest of year.

JÖNKÖPING. Riddersberg Manor. In Rogberga, 10 km. (six miles) east of Jönköping. Huge wooden sculptures in a park, such as the 103-meter (338-ft.) high *Indian Rope Trick* and the *Bounty* (a ship on land). *The Giant Vist,* another sculpture by the same artist, Calle Örnemark, is visible from the road at Huskvarna. The artist lives on the premises and sometimes conducts guided tours himself. Open daily 10–6. Admission free.

Dr. Skora's Vaxkabinett. Grännavägen 24, Huskvarna (036-142080). Life-size wax figures, which move, sing and speak. Cafeteria with view of Lake Vättern. Open daily during summer 10–7. Other times by agreement.

Tändsticksmuseet (Match Museum). Storgatan 18 (036-10 55 43). Match manufacturing started here in Jönköping in the middle of last century and made the city famous. Here in the original factory are machines and exhibits showing the development of the match industry. 13-minute film *The Match.* Large collection of match-box labels. Open June through Aug., Mon. to Fri. 10–6, Sat. 11–1, Sun. 3–5; Sept. through Dec., Sat. 11–1, Sun. 2–5.

KARLSKOGA. Nobelmuseet. Björkborn. The Alfred Nobel residence, including library, study and laboratory with original equipment. Open June through Aug., daily 10–4, Tues. and Thurs. also 7–9 P.M. On request at other times. Call 0586 818 94.

KATRINEHOLM. Julita Gård. On Lake Öljar, 25 km. (16 miles) north of Katrineholm. Typical turn-of-the-century manor house with parks and gardens. A homestead museum, dairy museum and the Skansen church. Museums open mid-May to mid-Aug., daily 11–4. Main building, guided tours only. For information call 0150-912 90 or 08-22 41 20.

MALMKÖPING. Museispårväg. Vintage tramway. 75-year-old tram on which you can take a half-hour trip. Tram museum, road museum. Open mid-June to mid-Aug., daily 11–5; May and Sept. on Sat. and Sun. only.

MARIEFRED. Gripsholm Castle. Castle was begun in 1370s. Among the many interesting things is an 18th-century theater. National portrait collection is here, one of largest in Europe. Modern portraits are in school building nearby. Boats from Stockholm. Open May through Aug., daily 10–4; Feb. through Apr., Tues. to Fri. 10–3, Sat. and Sun. 12–3; Dec. and Jan. open Sun. only, 12–3.

Östra Södermanlands Järnväg. Veteran railway operating between Mariefred and Läggesta during summer months. Call 0159-110 06 for timetable.

MORA. Zorn Museum. Vasagatan 36. Original paintings, sketches and sculptures of Swedish artist Anders Zorn. Open June 15 to Aug. 15, Mon. to Sat. 9–5; Sun. 11–5.

Zorngården. Adjoining museum. Zorn's home 1896–1920. In unchanged condition with silver collection, art, furniture etc. Guided tours every half-hour. Open June 15 to Aug. 15, Mon. to Sat. 10–5; Sun. 11–5.

ÖREBRO. Wadköping. In Stadsparken, 1.5 km. (a mile) from the center of town. Open-air museum. Old Town of Örebro with old wooden houses, streets and squares, handicrafts, workshops, exhibitions. Cafeteria. Open daily 12–5.

SUNNE. Mårbacka. Östra Ämtervik, 10 km. (six miles) south of Sunne. The home of Nobel prize winner (1909) Selma Lagerlöf. (Most of her books are available in English and German). Manor house in unchanged condition. Cafeteria. Guided tours—for information call 0565-310 27. Open May to Aug. daily 9–6; Sept., Sat. and Sun. only 9–6.

Rottneros Manor. 3 km. (two miles) south of Sunne. One of Sweden's most beautiful gardens with flowers, herb garden, sculptures and a wonderful view of Lake Fryken. Open May to Sept. daily 9–6; July, daily 8–7.

NORRLAND AND LAPLAND

Europe's Last Wilderness

The Swedish highlands, ranging from central Sweden up beyond the Arctic Circle for a distance of 800 kilometers (500 miles) or more, offer you holidays quite unlike any others anywhere; this is truly Europe's last wilderness. The region has been settled for centuries, its natural resources are among the most important in northern Europe, yet it is a country of open spaces, virgin wilderness, and a combination of natural beauties not to be found anywhere else in the world.

Norrland—as the entire region of northern Sweden is called—occupies half of Sweden's territory but holds only 17 per cent of its population. Modern industry already has put its stamp on parts of Norrland, with its vast resources of timber, iron ore, and water power. But the traditional peasant culture of the river valleys and coastal areas, deep-rooted in the Middle Ages, and the ageless civilization of the independent, nomadic Lapps have remained virtually unchanged.

This area has its charm at all seasons of the year and offers a variety of delights to lovers of the outdoors. From Christmas to May skiing predominates. If the winters are long, the summers are brilliant—the countryside bursts into bloom, temperatures of 80–85°F (27–29°C) are not unusual, and the "sunlit nights" merge day into day with only a few hours of twilight between. In the far north, the Midnight Sun sees to it that there is no night at all from May 25 to July 15.

Härjedalen

Sandwiched between Norway in the west, Jämtland in the north, the coastal provinces in the east, and Dalarna in the south, Härjedalen possesses only one center of any size—Sveg, with a little over 4,000 inhabitants. Because of this—or in spite of it—Härjedalen was the first mountain province to attract visitors in the days when both tourism and skiing were in their infancy. One reason for its continued popularity with skiers is the great variety of terrain it offers, from the gentle rounded southern mountains to the originally volcanic Helag Mountains in the north. Fjällnäs, Funäsdalen, Bruksvallarna and Vemdalskalet all offer comfortable lodging and are both summer and winter resorts.

Across the Flatruet plateau in the western part of the province runs the highest road in Sweden (914 meters or 3,000 feet), offering a breathtaking view from its summit. On one of the cliff walls are rock paintings, almost 4,000 years old, depicting animal and human figures. Another curiosity is the "frozen sea" of the Rogen area, with its striated and pitted Ice Age boulders.

Jämtland

Östersund is on the railroad line that crosses the Scandinavian peninsula from Sundsvall, industrial center on the east coast of Sweden, to Trondheim on Norway's Atlantic coast, a fact which accounts for much of its growth in recent years. Despite its northerly clime, however, the region around Storsjön, or the Great Lake, has been settled since heathen times. The ancient capital of this region was Frösön, an island in the lake just off what is now Östersund. It was the site of a heathen sacrificial temple and the place where the *ting*, or popular council, met. The strange Viking alphabet also penetrated here, and the northernmost rune stone in Sweden is to be found on Frösön near the bridge. It was erected there by one Östman Gudfastsson about the year 1050. From the heights of Frösön you have unbelievably distant views —of the lake, the cultivated areas around the shores, and, in the west, the mountains reaching above the timberline.

Today Östersund has taken over Frösön's role as capital of the province, and has grown into a city of 56,000 inhabitants, with several industries. It is a good starting point for motor tours within the province or into Norway—the joint Swedish-Norwegian "Trondheimsleden" highway leads via Enafors and Storlien to Trondheim.

Here are some of the principal resorts in the region stretching west of Östersund:

Åre, site of a former World Ski Championship, and located in the beautiful Åre valley at the foot of the Åreskutan mountain, is popular both winter and summer. It is the largest resort in this region and also boasts a church dating from the 12th or 13th century.

There are a dozen or so other resorts or mountain hotels, among them Duved, Undersåker, Hålland, Ånn, Bydalen, and Anjan, all with good terrain. Farther north, in even more isolated country, are Gäddede and Jormlien. You're really in the wilderness here—observe reasonable precautions before taking off from your hotel. There are expert guides. The requirement that you notify the management of your intended route when you go out any distance is a simple precaution for your own safety. Don't laugh at it. Even if you're in perfect safety, which is likely, you'll feel awfully silly if half the population drops its other pursuits to come out looking for you.

Gästrikland and Hälsingland

Going north along the coast you reach the regions of Gästrikland and Hälsingland. The provincial capital is Gävle, a town with a busy harbor on the Baltic. Gävle's "old section" still has the small wooden houses of former times, and a castle built in 1613. Further on, 80 kilometers (50 miles) from Gävle, is the veteran Jädraås-Tallås railway. Here the traveler can enjoy a landscape of forest and lake, and a coastline dotted with bays, inlets and islands.

Hälsingland is known throughout Sweden for the world's largest folk dancing competition, with 1,500 couples competing. It is held in July in Hårga, Bollnäs, Arbrå and Järvsö. A visit to Järvsö should also be relished for the magnificence of its scenery. The manor houses to be seen in this area are generally large and memorable. Characterized by folklore and handicraft products, this country's culinary specialty is smoked Baltic herring, called "böckling."

Medelpad and Ångermanland

Here, in a region also known as Västernorrland, you are right in the middle of Sweden: Flataklacken at Torpshammar is actually the geographical center. You will encounter stretches of coast here that are quite different from the rest of the country. On the Höga Kusten, or High Coast, at Nordingrå, steep hills rise straight out of the sea and the inlets would be better described as fjords.

The rivers are also distinctive features of the landscape, with the Indal and Ångerman Rivers being the most impressive. On the Indal there is a 72-kilometer (45-mile) long channel for canoeing with rustic overnight cabins. There are many hiking trails in this area. An important beaver colony can be found near Ramsele.

Near Sundsvall is Alnön, known for its unusual geological features. From neighbouring Härnösand, a pleasant town with old-world charms, and Örnsköldsvik you can take a boat trip to Trysunda and Ulvön, which is known as the "Pearl of the Baltic." The view from the 350-meter (1,150-foot) high "Skuleberget" is fantastic. A chair lift operates from Docksta.

Västerbotten—the Gateway to Lapland

The road from Umeå is called Blå Vägen, or the Blue Route (E79). This beautiful road goes all the way to the Atlantic. Other parallel routes have names like the Silver Road, the Saga Road and the Road of the Seven Rivers. The Stekenjokk Road goes from Vilhelmina over bare mountains to the province of Jämtland.

Along the coast at Lövånger are more than a hundred timber cottages dating from the 17th century. They are now renovated and available for tourists to stay in. At Lycksele on the Blue Route there is a large zoo featuring Nordic animals. Also Gammelplatsen—an outdoor museum—and a pretty 18th-century church.

Lapland

There is nothing more dramatic in all of Scandinavia than this region north of the Arctic Circle. It seems terribly far north, terribly distant, and it is at about the same latitude as northern Alaska. Yet it is a remarkably accessible place. You climb aboard an express train in Stockholm one afternoon, sleep soundly in a comfortable sleeper, eat in the diner, and by noon the next day you have arrived in a strange and wonderful world. (The flight from Stockholm to Kiruna takes 90 minutes.)

These contradictions never fail to fascinate the visitor. The region is huge—the province of Lapland covers about one fourth of Sweden's total area, but is only sparsely settled, of course. And its great beauty as a vacation region is the ease and comfort with which you reach it, without strain, special clothes or equipment, or much traveling time.

If you travel by train, the main line proceeds on or near the eastern coast, along the Gulf of Bothnia, all the way to the city of Boden. You pass through a huge industrial region—largely forest products—and magnificent natural scenery. Since this is a night train you will sleep through most of it, but the coastal cities, such as Gävle, a major port; Sundsvall, a paper and pulp center; Umeå, the cultural capital of northern Sweden; and Luleå, with a museum featuring Lapp collections and a 15th-century church, are of more than passing interest. Outside Luleå there is an archipelago of 300 islands.

The whole of northern Sweden is a region of forests and huge rivers. The rivers cut eastward across country from the mountain range along the Norwegian border to the east coast of Sweden, and are used both to float logs to factories on the Baltic coast and for hydro-electric power. A trip through this region shows you why Sweden is one of the world's great producers of paper, woodpulp, and other wood products —the forests seem endless. At Boden, a northern military and industrial hub, the line makes a junction with the line going diagonally across Norrland, from Luleå on the Swedish coast to Narvik, Norway. It was built around the turn of the century to exploit the huge finds of iron ore (up to 70 per cent pure) at Gällivare and Kiruna. Narvik, an ice-free port, has become the principal shipping point, and Luleå ranks second. Up to 16,000,000 tons of ore are taken out and shipped annually via this line, and the ore trains run day and night.

The coast at Piteå is called the Riviera of the North; there is a lot of sun here in summer and the water is sometimes as warm as the water in the Mediterranean. This is a favorite vacation spot for Norwegians from northern Norway, since the water in the Atlantic is much colder.

North of the Arctic Circle

Keep your eyes open after you leave Boden. About 97 kilometers (60 miles) north—and a little west—you will see a line of white stones cutting squarely across the railroad tracks and a sign "Arctic Circle" in two or three languages, including English. You're now in the land of the Midnight Sun, near the legendary home of Santa Claus.

The sun never sets from the end of May until the middle of July, and if you have looked at pictures of it making its way across the horizon, let us assure you at once they are misleading. The apparent darkness in the photos, giving more of an impression of moonlight than sunlight, is caused by the filters used when shooting directly at the sun. Actually, the Midnight Sun is as bright as it is anywhere an hour or so before sunset. The whole thing has a mystical, unreal, ethereal quality—you sometimes find yourself feeling almost light headed. But well before the date when the sun actually stays above the horizon all night and well afterwards, the nights are light all night long. So if your visit must take place a week or two before or after the specific dates given, you will still enjoy the "sunlit nights" that give you approximately the same sensation.

64 kilometers (40 miles) north of Boden you arrive in Gällivare, center of a mining region with ore reserves estimated at 400,000,000 tons. The principal mine is Malmberget, about four miles out of town. From here you can take an interesting side trip, the railway to Porjus and then by a new road to Vietas, not far from the Saltoluokta Tourist Station, and from there a motorboat trip in Sjöfallsleden, "Lapland's Blue Ribbon", the source lakes of the Big Lule River. Combined with some 19 kilometers (12 miles) walking you will, by this westbound route, finally reach the Atlantic. At Gällivare you will get the first glimpse of the Lapland mountains. Dundret (Thunder Mountain), 760 meters (2,500 feet), has a convenient chair lift to its summit, and the view is well worth the trip. The midnight sun is visible in this neighborhood from June 1 to July 12.

Kiruna

Another 80 kilometers (50 miles) or so north on the main railway line is Kiruna, the world's biggest city in terms of area. Kiruna became big enough to accommodate, shall we say, London, New York, and a few dozen other cities by incorporating the whole province within the municipality some years ago. It covers no less than 4,800 square kilometers (3,000 square miles), about the same size as the province of Skåne. The mining town proper had a population of some 21,000, but only picked up an additional 6,000 or so people by this huge extension of its borders. The people, including the Lapps, were quick to react to the knowledge that they were living in the world's biggest city. A man we know was trying to get hold of a Lapp friend of his by telephone to a remote village. He finally succeeded in locating the man's wife, who said her husband wasn't at home: "He's out in the city with the reindeer herd."

Kiruna lies on a slope between two ore-bearing mountains with the jaw-cracking names of Kirunavaara and Luossavaara. The ore reserves are estimated at 500,000,000 tons. Mining operations are going more and more underground, but during the past decades most ore has been taken out by the open-cast method. You should try to see the biggest pit—if possible when blasting is going on. Tons of dynamite go off at one time in a huge manifestation of explosive power. From high points around Kiruna you get beautiful views—on clear days you can see the irregular contours of Kebnekaise, Sweden's highest mountain, about 80 kilometers (50 miles) away. And here in Kiruna you may see the blue and red costumes of the Lapps for the first time.

Meeting the Lapps

For a long time the Lapps were believed to be of Mongolian origin, but the latest theory now supposes they stem from somewhere in central Europe. Presumably they came to northern Scandinavia more than 1,000 years ago. They number about 8,000 in Sweden (of whom only 2,000 are nomads deriving a living from the breeding of reindeer), 20,000 in Norway, 2,500 in Finland, and perhaps less than 2,000 in the Soviet Union.

The reindeer is the bone, sinew, and marrow of the economy of the nomadic Lapps of this area. (There are also forest Lapps and fishing Lapps.) Reindeer is the only domestic animal which can feed itself on the meager vegetation here beyond the Arctic Circle. The Lapps are nomads perhaps less from a restless desire to keep on the move than from the necessity of following their reindeer herds from one grazing ground to another. In the winter they move down to the protected forests, east and south of the mountains, but in the spring they travel in the opposite direction for the grazing on the high slopes. The total number of reindeer in the Swedish herds has been estimated at something like 200,000.

The Lapp culture is not as primitive as many have chosen to believe —rather, it is a highly developed culture perfectly adapted to perhaps the only way of life which will mean independent survival in these northern wastes. Take just the matter of languages, for example: practically all of the Lapps are at least bi-lingual and many are fluent in three or four tongues—their own language, Swedish, Norwegian, Finnish, and possibly others. Their handicrafts make use of the horns and skins of reindeer, and their distinctive costumes, largely in red, yellow, and blue, are as functional as they are ornamental. During the war they performed invaluable services to the Allied cause by helping Norwegians and other prisoners of the Nazis escape from Norway through the mountains to Sweden.

The Lapps, as they follow their herds, live in a special type of tepee, or hut, which is called a *kåta*. They eat reindeer meat—some reindeer are milked—and about the only things a Lapp family needs from the outside world are coffee and salt. They, like other people in the North, are devoted to coffee. Some of the larger reindeer owners are wealthy. Many now move to and from the summer camps by helicopter, leaving only the young men to accompany the herds. But don't ask a Lapp how many reindeer he has. It is the measure of his wealth, and is about as rude and nosy a question as asking an acquaintance how much money he has.

The Lapps have equal status with other Swedes under the law, and some special privileges. The government provides special schools for their education, and attendance is compulsory, as it is for all the other groups. There is a special inn for Lapps in Kiruna, and you may see them on the streets. Or you may meet them on the train carrying knapsacks. Don't be patronizing—they're not "simple" people. They have produced at least one great primitive artist and some university professors. But whatever their talents, whatever their education, most of them prefer their own way of life. You may get some idea of the traditional Lapp way of life by visiting the "Lappstaden" at Arvidsjaur, an old village of 70 cone-shaped Lapp huts which are still used for church visits at festival times.

Jukkasjärvi

Almost due east of Kiruna, about 15 to 25 kilometers (ten or 15 miles), is Jukkasjärvi, a little village. This is a sort of semi-permanent

Lapp headquarters, with a modern school, an equally modern home for aged Lapps, and an appealing old church. The structure dates from 1726, was built on the site of a previous church (1611) which was the second one in all of Lapland. Note the remarkable architecture. At the times of the great religious holidays, Lapps gather here in huge crowds, and a Lapp wedding may be a tremendous event.

To get to Jukkasjärvi you must cross the mighty Torne River. These rushing waters make a magnificent sight, and beneath the turbulent surface there are fighting game fish—including salmon, trout, and grayling.

At Kaitum, 24 kilometers (15 miles) south of Kiruna is the Kaitum Chapel consecrated in 1964 as an ecclesiastical center for Laplanders but also as a memorial to Dag Hammarskjöld, the Swedish-born Secretary General of the United Nations.

Mount Kebnekajse, 2,123 meters (6,965 feet) above sea level, the highest mountain in Sweden, is an excursion point best reached from Kiruna. It is really in the wilderness, about 32 kilometers (20 miles) by bus, 40 (25 miles) by motorboat, and the last 24 (15 miles) on foot. (In the winter it's bus and skis; sometimes sleighs are available.) Here you literally get away from it all, but the trip is recommended only for those who are in good physical condition. From Kebnekaise the sun is visible round the clock from May 23 to July 22.

An hour or so north of Kiruna on the main railway line you approach the southern shore of Lake Torneträsk, a long, narrow body of water which extends for miles almost to the Norwegian border. This is the real wilderness, but modern communications put it right outside your window. The railroad and the new road follow the southern shore, and at the eastern end you come to one of the most popular resort regions in Lapland.

The first resort, and the best known, that you reach is Abisko. There are regular motorboat tours on Lake Torneträsk, mountain excursions during the summer season and skiing during the spring. The sun is visible round the clock from June 12 to July 4. Björkliden is a few kilometers farther along, also on the railway line, located near Lake Torneträsk. About eight kilometers (five miles) away is Låktatjåkko.

The very last resort before you cross into Norway is Riksgränsen (the frontier). The little railway station also serves as the customs house. Here you can enjoy skiing by the light of the Midnight Sun, which shines from May 26 to July 18.

PRACTICAL INFORMATION FOR THE NORTH

TOURIST INFORMATION. There are tourist offices in the following places: **Åre,** Torget (0647- 500 10). **Bräcke** (0693–100 00). **Dorotea,** Torget (0942–112 06). **Funäsdalen** (0684–21420). **Gäddede** (0672–105 00). **Gäyle,** Norra Strandgatan 11–13 (026–10 16 00). **Hammarstrand** (0696–102 73). **Hede** (0684–110 80). **Kiruna,** Bus Station (0980–188 80). **Luleå,** Rådstugatan 9 (0920 –937 46). **Östersund,** Rådstugatan 9 (063–14 40 01). **Skellefteå,** Storgatan 46 (0910–772 60). **Sollefteå,** Storgatan 59 (0620–143 67). **Sundsvall,** Torget (060– 11 42 35). **Sveg** (0680–107 75). **Tärnaby,** Blå Vägen 30 (0954–103 00). **Umeå,** Renmarkstorget (090–16 16 16). **Vemdalen** (0684–302 70).

TELEPHONE CODES. We have given telephone codes for all the towns and villages in the hotel and restaurant lists that follow. These codes need only be used when calling from outside the town or village concerned.

HOTELS AND RESTAURANTS. North, south and west of Östersund, the mountain resorts of Jämtland are concentrated. These are not generally luxury establishments: they are designed principally for people who like the outdoors, and the rates are reasonable. In Lapland, you will find both modest hotels and modern, comfortable tourist hotels.

ÅRE. *Diplomat-Åregarden* (E) (0647–502 65). 41 rooms; open Nov. to May. *Åre Fjällby* (I), (0647–504 50). 70 flats. 800 meters (880 yards) to railway station. Sauna, pool, gym, restaurants, dancing. Near ski lifts. Open year-round. AE, DC, MC, V. *Åregården* (I), 109 rooms. 400 meters (1,312 ft.) above sea level. 100 meters (328 ft.) to cable lift and railway station. Sauna, pool, dancing. Sports equipment for rent. Open year-round. AE, MC, V. *Sunwing Åre* (I) (0647-504 30). 50 rooms, 102 flats. Restaurant, dancing, nightclub, cafeteria. Sauna, pool, ski lift. AE, DC, MC, V.

ARVIDSJAUR. *Laponia* (M), (0960–108 80). 118 rooms. Restaurant, nightclub, saunas, pool. AE, DC, MC, V.

BJÖRKLIDEN. *Hotel Fjället* (I) (0980-410 50). 70 rooms, 80 cottages. On railway and road to Swedish border. 500 meters (1,640 ft.) above sea level. Overlooking majestic mountain and Lake Torneträsk. Midnight Sun May 31 to July 16. Pension. Restaurant, dancing. Saunas, ski lifts. Excursions summer and winter. Open Feb. to middle Sept. (bookings 08–24 83 60). AE, MC, V.

BORGAFJÄLL, S. LAPPLAND. *Hotel Borgafjäll* (I) (0942-420 16). 30 chalet-type rooms. 540 meters (1,772 ft.) above sea level. Bus to Dorotea. Restaurant, sauna, slalom, fishing. Also self-service cottages. Open Feb. 15 to Apr. 30 and middle June through Sept. AE, MC, V.

BRUKSVALLARNA, HÄRJEDALEN. *Ramundbergets Fjällgård* (I) (0684-270 10). 58 rooms. Nine km. (five miles) to Bruksvallarna. 750 meters (2,460 ft.) above sea level. Restaurant, dancing. Sauna, indoor pool, ski lifts, excursions, fishing. Open Dec. to beginning May and July through Sept. MC, V.

DOROTEA. *Hotel Dorotea* (M), (0942-10810). 29 rooms. Excellent cuisine. Try *Hubbes Horrible Hash,* mountain lake char *a la Raukasjö.* AE, DC, MC.

GÄVLE. *Grand Central* (M), Nygatan 45 (026-12 90 60). 240 rooms. Central. Restaurants *Trägårn* and *Skeppet* with marine atmosphere. Dancing, nightclub. AE, DC, MC, V. *Hotel Gävle* (M), Norra Slottsgatan 9 (026–17 70 00). 200 rooms. Pleasant atmosphere. Cafe Artist restaurant. Piano bar. AE, DC, MC, V.

Restaurants. *Skeppet* (the Ship) (M), Nygatan 45 (026-12 90 60). In 100-year-old cellar vaults. Fresh *strömming* (Baltic herring) in all variations. MC, V. *Strandgården* (M), at Bönan fishing village, 13 km. (eight miles) north of Gävle (026-992 80). View of the sea. Fish, especially *strömming.* MC, V.

HAMMARSTRAND. *Gullbacken* (I), (0696–107 80). 30 rooms, 22 cabins. Pool, sauna, restaurant. Open year-round. MC.

HÄRNÖSAND. *Sara Statt* (M), Skeppsbron 9 (0611–105 10). 76 rooms. Restaurant, cocktail bar, dancing, sauna. AE, MC, V.

Restaurant. *Gastgiveri Spiutegården* (M). Murberget (0611–110 99). Inn dating from 1801. At the open-air museum, on a mountain with a view of the harbor; two km. (1.2 miles) from the center of town. MC, V.

HEMAVAN, Lappland. *Hemavan Fjällhotell* (Mountain Resort Hotel) (0954 –301 50). 72 rooms. 500 meters (1,640 ft.) above sea level. Pension. Restaurant, sauna. Ski lifts, helicopter lift, marked trails, canoes etc. Open Christmas to mid-May and early-June to mid-Sept. AE, DC, MC, V.

KIRUNA. *Ferrum* (M), Köpmangatan 1 (0980-186 00). 170 rooms. 510 meters (1,673 ft.) above sea level. Restaurant, cocktail bar, saunas. Also 90 flats at *Ripan.* AE, DC, MC, V.

Youth Hostel. Strandstigen (0980-171 95). 90 beds. 500 meters (546 yards) from bus stop and railway station. Open June 15 through Aug.

LULEÅ. *SAS Lulea* (M), Storgatan 17 (0920-940 00). 213 rooms. SAS office, airport bus. Restaurant *Cooks Krog,* nightclub, sauna, solarium. AE, DC, MC, V. *Scandic* (M), Mjölkudden (0920-283 60). 164 rooms. Restaurant, sauna, solarium, airport bus. AE, DC, MC, V.

ÖSTERSUND. *Hotel Östersund* (M), Kyrkgatan 70 (063–11 76 40). 129 rooms. Central. Sauna, restaurant, dancing, nightclub. AE, DC, MC, V. *Winn* (M), Prästgatan 16 (063-12 77 40). 198 rooms. Central, airport bus. Restaurant *Stadshuskällaren,* dancing, sauna. AE, MC, V.

Youth Hostel. Tingsgatan 12 (063–12 85 61). 100 beds. Open end June to beginning Aug.

STORA BLÅSJÖN. *Blåsjöns Fjällhotel* (I), (0672–210 40). 30 rooms and flats and 16 cabins. Sauna, restaurant, outdoor activities, near ski lifts. Open July to Sept., Dec. to Apr. AE, MC, V.

STORLIEN. *Storliens Högfjällshotel* (I), (0647–701 70). 200 rooms, 34 cabins. Sauna, pool, restaurant, dancing, near ski lifts. Open year-round except May to June. AE, DC, MC, V.

SUNDSVALL. *Sundsvall* (M), Esplanaden 29 (060-17 16 00). 203 rooms. Restaurant, dancing, sauna. AE, DC, MC, V.

Restaurants. *Oskar* (M), Vängåvan (060-12 98 11). Central. French cuisine and Nordic fare. MC, V. *Turistpaviljongen* (I), Norra Stadsberget (060-11 42 22). On a mountain-top with an excellent view of the city. Three km. (two miles) from the center. MC, V.

Youth Hostel. Gaffelbyn (060-11 21 19). 155 beds. 2.5 km. (1.6 miles) from center of town, on hill. Open all year.

TÄNNDALEN. *Hamrafjällets Högsfjällshotel* (I), (0684–230 00). 55 rooms. Four km. (three miles) west of Tänndalen. Sauna, restaurant. Open Dec. to Apr., June to Oct. AE, MC.

UMEÅ. *Blå Aveny* (E), Rådhusesplanaden 14 (090-13 23 00). 165 rooms. Central. Restaurant, cocktail bar, dancing, pub. Sauna, peaceful atmosphere. AE, DC, MC, V. *Blå Dragonen* (Blue Dragon) (M), Norrlandsgatan 5 (090-13 23 80). 71 rooms. Central. Steakhouse *Ryttmästaren* (Cavalry Captain) and restaurant *Blå Dragonen.* Dancing, sauna, heated outdoor pool, sun terrace. AE, DC, MC, V.

Restaurants. *Sävargården* (E), at the open-air museum Gammlia, five minutes by car from center (090-11 02 22). Dates from 18th century. Headquarters of the Russian General Kamenski for a time during the 1808–9 war. *Smörgåsbord,* with food from Västerbotten. AE, MC, V. *Cajsa Warg* (I),

Kungsgatan 52 (090-12 44 22). Central. Steakhouse. Specialties from area. During day self-service, at night table service. AE, MC, V.

Youth Hostel. Åliden (090-12 57 60). 100 beds. Three km. (two miles) from railway station. Bus 8. Open June through August.

Camping

There are over 200 camping sites in this area. Many of them have log cabins and chalets for rent and most of them can be reached by bus or train: **Bollnäs,** Orbaden, Vallsta (0278-455 63). 24 chalets. On Lake Orsjön. Bus 500 meters (546 yards). Near ski lifts. Bike, canoe rentals. Open all year. **Delsbo,** *Delsbo Camping,* west of Delsbo on road 84 (0653-163 03). 4 chalets. On lake, 500 meters (546 yards) from bus stop. Canoes for rent. Open June 15 to Aug. 15. **Haparanda,** Kukkolaforsen (0922-310 00). 20 chalets. On route 99, 15 km. (nine miles) north of Haparanda. Restaurant, fishing, canoe safaris. Open all year. **Hede,** *Hede Camping* (0684-110 20). 15 chalets. On lake, excursions, boats, canoe rentals. Open all year. **Jokkmokk,** Kuossinjarka, Vaihijaur (097-310 13). 50 chalets. Bus stop, 12 km. (7.4 miles) from center. On lake. Bike, boat, canoe rentals. Open June to Aug. **Lycksele,** Ansia (0950-100 83). 38 chalets. On road 90 on east side of Umeå River, 1.5 km. (a mile) from town center. Bus 200 meters (200 yards). Canoe and bike rentals. Open June through Aug. **Luleå,** *Luleå Camping* at Skogsvallen (0920-932 64). 26 chalets. Central, bus stop, bike and canoe rentals. Open June to Aug. **Nordingrå,** Norrfällsviken, 30 km. (19 miles) from E4 (0613-213 82). 20 chalets. Canoes for rent. Open June 18 through Aug. **Östersund,** Fritidsby, Odenslingan 831, on E75 (063-11 37 06). 112 cabins. Central. Open all year. **Skellefteå,** *Skelleftea Camping,* on E4 (0910-188 55). 34 chalets. 14 km. (8.6 miles) north of town center. Sauna, ski lift; bikes for rent. Open all year. **Storuman,** *Storuman Camping,* 200 meters (220 yards) south of Blue Route (0951-106 96). 22 cabins. On lake. Sauna; boats and canoes for rent. Open June through Aug. **Sundsvall/Härnösand,** Bye Rast, Söråker, on E4 (060-450 55). 20 chalets. 38 km. (24 miles) north of Sundsvall. Canoes and boats for rent. Open all year. **Undersåker,** Ristafallet, on Indal River (0647-311 10). 8 cabins. 400 meters (440 yards) south of E75 and seven km. (4.3 miles) west of Järpen. Waterfall. Open June through Aug.

HOW TO GET AROUND. By car. The most important route to northern Sweden, Highway E4, continues from Stockholm to Haparanda on the Finnish border—1,134 km. (705 miles). The main routes to the interior highlands branch off this highway at Hudiksvall: road 84 via Sveg to Funäsdalen— 322 km. (200 miles); Sundsvall: E75 via Östersund to Åre—300 km. (186 miles) and Storlien, so further into Norway to Trondheim; at Umeå: roads 92, 93 and 361—the very scenic Blå Vägen—through Storuman to Tärnaby and Hemavan, and on to Mo i Rana, below the Arctic Circle; at Luleå: roads 97 and 98 via Jokkmokk and Gällivare to Kiruna—381 km. (237 miles).

The new "Norgevägen" (Norway Route) from Kiruna to Narvik is now open. It passes through upland marshes and gently-rolling hills which rise up gradually to the mountains near the Norwegian border at Riksgränsen, from which the road makes a quick descent to the coast. Another route leading into Norway goes from Vilhelmina along the beautiful Lake Vojmsjön to Dikanäs and Kittelfjäll and via the frontier village of Skalmodal to Mosjöen in Norway—400 km. (248 miles).

Note that it is forbidden to take photographs near the defense areas of Sundsvall and Kalix on Highway E4, and Boden on Highway 97.

By train. Two main rail lines traverse Sweden in a south-north direction: from Stockholm near the coast to the Finnish border, and the Inlandsbanan (inland railway) from Dalarna province through the interior to Gällivare. The Inlandsbanan runs for more than 1,120 km. (696 miles) from Kristinehamn via Mora and Östersund to Gällivare. Part of the run is by bus. During the summer a discount ticket is offered for two or three weeks' unlimited travel on the line. Among other sites, the train stops at the Arctic Circle south of Jokkmokk. An Arctic Circle or *Polcirkel* certificate is sold at the tourist office in Jokkmokk.

The Sundsvall-Trondheim and Luleå-Narvik lines cross it in an east-west direction. Secondary lines and postal buses, fanning out from the railroad stations, supplement this network and make even remote districts conveniently accessible. From Stockholm it is 6½ hours to Östersund by express train, 9 to Storlien, 14 to Luleå, 18 to Kiruna and19½ to Abisko.

By bus. Long-distance buses link Stockholm and Gothenburg with Funäsdalen and Sundsvall with Luleå. Swedish State Railways also offers nine-day guided bus tours of the North Cape twice weekly from mid-June to mid-August, starting at Luleå and ending at Narvik in Norway. RESO operates a seven-day North Cape tour starting and ending in Kiruna daily from early June to mid-August.

By air. There are airports at Gävle, Östersund, Sundsvall, Kramfors, Skellefteå, Umeå, Luleå, Gällivare and Kiruna. You can fly from Stockholm to Sundsvall in 45 minutes, to Umeå in 60 minutes, to Luleå in 75 minutes, to Östersund in 55 minutes, to Kiruna in 90 minutes. SAS and Scandinavian Express operate a weekly "Midnight Sun Excursion" from early June through Aug. 10. You fly from Stockholm to Kiruna and continue by road to Riksgränsen for an evening excursion to Narvik on the Norwegian coast and a mountain-top view of the Midnight Sun, returning to Stockholm the following day.

By ferry. If your preference is for a more leisurely route, there is a car ferry service from Vaasa in Finland to Sundsvall (11 hours) and Umeå (3½ hours), and from Pietarsaari in Finland to Skellefteå (5 hours).

 PLACES TO VISIT. Wilderness, forests and mountains are not the whole story. Among the other sights at the far north of Sweden are:

ARJEPLOG. Silvermuseet. Storgatan 20. Large collection of Lapp handicrafts and silver; 600-year-old tools and fireplaces, and much more. Open Mon. to Fri. 11–3, Sat. and Sun. 12–3. In summer, longer opening hours. Adm. free.

HÄRNÖSAND. Murberget Homestead Museum. 1.5 km. (a mile) from center of town. Old farmhouses from the area; church, shop, school from 19th century. Tour every day. Demonstrations of spinning, weaving etc. weekly—for information on tours call 0611-232 40. Open June to Aug. 15, daily 10–4. Admission free.

Länsmuseet (Provincial Museum). Near Murberget. Has archeological finds, handicrafts etc. and is open same times as Homestead Museum.

JOKKMOKK. Jokkmokk Museum. Kyrkogatan. Also called the "Arctic Circle Museum." Lapp handicrafts and silver. Exhibits showing the frontier life of settlers. Animals of the north. Open Mon. to Fri. 12–3, Sat. and Sun. 1–4; June through Aug., Mon. to Fri. 10–7, Sat. and Sun. 12–6.

JUKKASJÄRVI. Jukkasjärvi Homestead Museum. 17 km. (11 miles) south of Kiruna. Old farm, log cabins and many types of Lapp *kåta* (huts) and sheds. Beautiful altar painting in nearby wooden church. Cafeteria. Tour four times daily—call 0980-211 90 for times. Open June through Aug., daily 10–9.

ÖSTERSUND. Jamtli Open-Air Museum. Centrally placed. 18th century manor house, Lapp *kåta* (huts), town houses, market place etc. Mid-summer to Aug. there are activities in many of the buildings, daily 10–6. Park open all year. Small admission fee.

Jämtlands Läns Museum. Provincial museum close to Jamtli. Rich collections of folk art, paintings etc. Temporary exhibitions. Open Mon. to Fri. 10–4, Sat. and Sun. 12–5. Admission free.

STORFORSEN. Skogsbruksmuseet (Forestry Museum). At Storforsen River, 40 km. (25 miles) west of Älvsbyn. Permanent exhibition of forestry and timber-floating through the ages. Charcoal and tar are occasionally made here in the traditional way. Tour three times daily—call 0929-310 91 for times of tours. Open June through Aug., daily 10–4. Admission free.

SUNDSVALL. Norra Berget (North Hill) Homestead Museum. Two km. (1.2 miles) from center of city (uphill). Buildings from the 19th century. Open Mon. to Fri. 10–4, Sat and Sun. 11–4; June through Aug., daily 9–7. Admission free.

Sundsvall Museum. Storgatan 29. Sawmill and city history. Finds from Iron Age, paintings etc. Temporary exhibitions. Open Mon. to Thurs. 11–8, Fri. to Sun. 11–4; summer, daily 11–4. Admission free.

SPORTS. Many well-marked trails for **hiking** and **climbing** criss-cross the entire mountain area. Most spectacular of these is the "King's Trail" (Kungsleden) leading from Jäckvik through the Sarek district north to Abisko. Kvikkjokk is the starting point for tours up the beautiful Tarra valley and can be conveniently reached from Jokkmokk. From Kiruna you can reach Nikkaluokta at the foot of 2,123-meter (6,965-ft) Mount Kebnekaise, Sweden's highest mountain, but experience of tough mountaineering, including snow and ice climbing, is essential. The "Jämtland Triangle", a large block of mountains to the west towards the Norwegian border, is a popular area for hiking. Storsylen reaches a height of 1,762 meters (5,780 ft.) and Sylarna is a jagged range with three small glaciers. An extensive network of mountain huts is maintained by the Swedish Touring Club, and expeditions with guides start regularly from the various tourist stations.

Fine possibilities for trout **fishing** exist throughout the region; also char, grayling, and salmon. Among the waterways, try the Dalälven, Ljungan, Indal, Ljusnan, and Torne rivers, and the "Ströms vattudal", nine connecting lakes stretching northwest from Strömsund to Frostviken. Other excellent fishing centers are Saxnäs, Tärnaby, Ammarnäs, and Arvidsjaur. Fishing license fees are low; for fishing in Jämtland waters write to the Tourist Office, Rådhusplan, S-83182 Östersund, and for fishing in Lapland to Norrbotten Tourist Board, S-951 84 Luleå, or to Västerbotten Länsturistnämnd, S-90107 Umeå.

Forests abound in game for the **hunter,** especially moose, particularly plentiful in Jämtland; open season: four days, usually starting the second Monday of September. Special permits are required for the import and export of rifles and ammunition, and expeditions are arranged for hunters from abroad; write to the Tourist Office, Rådhusplan, S-83182 Östersund.

WINTER SPORTS. The northland is **skiing** country— slalom and cross-country. The Swedes are specialists in cross-country, with a string of Olympic titles to prove the point. Härjedalen: Smallest of Sweden's four skiing provinces, also the highest; not quite as accessible as the others but very good skiing facilities, ski lifts in most resorts, and many good hotels; season in Fjällnäs district runs from January to mid-April. Jämtland: Sweden's most frequented winter resort area, thanks to its accessibility, facilities, and fine accommodation along Stockholm-Östersund-Trondheim railway; "snow weasels" are a feature, also torchlight sleigh rides, fishing through the ice, curling; season in Åre-Storlien district from January to mid-April. Lapland: Only distance from the capital and the lateness with which its season starts prevent this area from nosing out Jämtland as Sweden's top skiing region; this is purely skiing country —no ice sports or sleighing parties; the tree line is low, so there are plenty of open slopes; latitude is the greatest asset here and spring skiing the greatest delight—this is where you enjoy the sensation of skiing in the Midnight Sun; season in the Tärna district runs from March to early May, in Abisko district from March through May.

Informality is the keynote of Swedish winter resort life. There is no shortage of *après ski* activities in the larger resorts like Åre, but in general the accent is on good companionship, relaxing before open fires, and the opportunity of acquiring a mid-winter tan. A word of caution with respect to the latter: the late winter-spring sun here has an unsuspected power—take good sun-glasses and be careful generally about over-exposing your face and body. Here is a brief survey of the provinces with their resorts and facilities.

Härjedalen is sleigh-ride and cross-country skiing territory, with marked trails and sleeping huts enticing skiers to two or three-day excursions. Its chief resorts are all clustered together, on a U-shaped road starting on the Norwegian border at *Fjällnäs* (732 meters or 2,400 ft.) and then paralleling the Tännån River southeastward through *Hamrafjället* (732 meters or 2,400 ft.) and *Tänn-dalen* (695 meters or 2,280 ft.), after which it swings around northeastward, with *Funäsdalen* (663 meters or 2,175 ft.) in the center of the bottom of the U and then turns northwest, with the last of the principal resorts, *Bruksvallarna* (778 meters or 2,550 ft.) falling at about the middle of the upper line of the U. *Vemdalsskalet*, finally, lies a little apart farther eastwards and just on the border to Jämtland province. Ski lifts at Fjällnäs, Hamrafjället, Bruksvallarna, Tänn-dalen, Tännäs, Funäsdalen, Sveg, Lofsdalen and Vemdalsskalet.

Jämtland offers a bewildering richness of resorts. Its transportation key is *Östersund*, the main station on the Stockholm-Trondheim line, which, while not strictly a resort, can be used as a center from which to sally forth to skiing slopes in the vicinity. It has excellent skating rinks. The most easily accessible resorts are those on this rail line, which, starting from Östersund, are *Hålland* and *Undersåker*, both with ski lifts; *Åre*, the chief winter sports center of Jämtland, with an overhead cable railway, several ski lifts and skating and curling rinks; *Duved* with new chair lift; *Ånn;* and *Storlien,* the second largest resort, which has a jump, ski lifts, slalom runs, one of which drops 235 meters (770 ft.) in a distance of 999 meters (3,280 ft.), ski schools for adults and children and skating rinks.

Another important area hugs the frontier south of Storlien, which gets you into some fairly high altitudes. First comes *Blåhammarstugan* (1,084 meters or 3,560 ft.). Southeast lies *Storulvåstugan* (730 meters or 2,395 ft.), south of that *Sylstugorna* (951 meters or 3,120 ft.), with a ski camp built another 91 meters (300 ft.) above it; and a little more than a few kilometers more to the south is the province's highest peak, *Mount Sylarna* (2,066 meters or 6,780 ft.). Of these resorts, Storulvåstugan has slalom runs and ski instructors on hand.

A few other resorts south of the main railway, between the border and Östersund, are worth mentioning. Farthest west, reached by road from Undersåker (on the rail line) is *Vålådalen,* a small popular resort with slalom and downhill runs, ski lift, a practice jump and a skating rink. Vålådalen is known as a training center for Sweden's Olympic cross-country skiers. About halfway between here and Östersund, and just about as far south of the railway, is *Bydalen,* with ski lift, and about as much farther south again, *Arådalen.* At *Hammarstrand,* some 97 km. (60 miles) east of Östersund, is a winter sports center with bobsleigh track, slalom run, ski lifts.

Lapland's most popular section is its farthest north, above the Arctic Circle. The entrance to this region is the iron-ore center of *Kiruna,* 200 km. (124 miles) north of the Arctic Circle. Kiruna is not itself a resort, but the nearby mountains provide slopes of all degrees of difficulty within easy reach, and by continuing through it on the Stockholm-Narvik railway or by road you pass in rapid succession through the three big winter sports centers of northern Lapland, all of which have slalom slopes, lifts, ski instructors and guides for the long excursions.

The first one reached from Kiruna is *Abisko* (310 meters or 1,020 ft.). A chair lift takes you up to the summit of Mount Nuolja with Midnight Sun from May 31 to July 16. Next comes *Björkliden,* which has a ski lift. Last station on the line, practically on the Norwegian border is *Riksgränsen,* also with a ski lift; the great attraction here is not simply sliding downhill from the top of the lift, but making excursions across the spectacular broad snowfields high up in the Riksgränsen mountains under the Midnight Sun.

There is also a winter sports center in southern Lapland around the resorts of Hemavan and Kittelfjäll. Ski lifts and good accommodation, but a little awkward to reach: direct train with sleepers from Stockholm to Storuman, then by bus.

Index

The letter H indicates Hotels and other accommodations.
The letter R indicates Restaurants.

FODOR'S TRAVEL GUIDES

Here is a complete list of Fodor's Travel Guides, available in current editions; most are also available in a British edition published by Hodder & Stoughton.

U.S. GUIDES

Alaska
American Cities (Great Travel Values)
Arizona including the Grand Canyon
Atlantic City & the New Jersey Shore
Boston
California
Cape Cod & the Islands of Martha's Vineyard & Nantucket
Carolinas & the Georgia Coast
Chesapeake
Chicago
Colorado
Dallas/Fort Worth
Disney World & the Orlando Area (Fun in)
Far West
Florida
Fort Worth (see Dallas)
Galveston (see Houston)
Georgia (see Carolinas)
Grand Canyon (see Arizona)
Greater Miami & the Gold Coast
Hawaii
Hawaii (Great Travel Values)
Houston & Galveston
I-10: California to Florida
I-55: Chicago to New Orleans
I-75: Michigan to Florida
I-80: San Francisco to New York
I-95: Maine to Miami
Jamestown (see Williamsburg)
Las Vegas including Reno & Lake Tahoe (Fun in)
Los Angeles & Nearby Attractions
Martha's Vineyard (see Cape Cod)
Maui (Fun in)
Nantucket (see Cape Cod)
New England
New Jersey (see Atlantic City)
New Mexico
New Orleans
New Orleans (Fun in)
New York City
New York City (Fun in)
New York State
Orlando (see Disney World)
Pacific North Coast
Philadelphia
Reno (see Las Vegas)
Rockies
San Diego & Nearby Attractions
San Francisco (Fun in)
San Francisco plus Marin County & the Wine Country
The South
Texas
U.S.A.
Virgin Islands (U.S. & British)
Virginia
Waikiki (Fun in)
Washington, D.C.
Williamsburg, Jamestown & Yorktown

FOREIGN GUIDES

Acapulco (see Mexico City)
Acapulco (Fun in)
Amsterdam
Australia, New Zealand & the South Pacific
Austria
The Bahamas
The Bahamas (Fun in)
Barbados (Fun in)
Beijing, Guangzhou & Shanghai
Belgium & Luxembourg
Bermuda
Brazil
Britain (Great Travel Values)
Canada
Canada (Great Travel Values)
Canada's Maritime Provinces plus Newfoundland & Labrador
Cancún, Cozumel, Mérida & the Yucatán
Caribbean
Caribbean (Great Travel Values)
Central America
Copenhagen (see Stockholm)
Cozumel (see Cancún)
Eastern Europe
Egypt
Europe
Europe (Budget)
France
France (Great Travel Values)
Germany: East & West
Germany (Great Travel Values)
Great Britain
Greece
Guangzhou (see Beijing)
Helsinki (see Stockholm)
Holland
Hong Kong & Macau
Hungary
India, Nepal & Sri Lanka
Ireland
Israel
Italy
Italy (Great Travel Values)
Jamaica (Fun in)
Japan
Japan (Great Travel Values)
Jordan & the Holy Land
Kenya
Korea
Labrador (see Canada's Maritime Provinces)
Lisbon
Loire Valley
London
London (Fun in)
London (Great Travel Values)
Luxembourg (see Belgium)
Macau (see Hong Kong)
Madrid
Mazatlan (see Mexico's Baja)
Mexico
Mexico (Great Travel Values)
Mexico City & Acapulco
Mexico's Baja & Puerto Vallarta, Mazatlan, Manzanillo, Copper Canyon
Montreal (Fun in)
Munich
Nepal (see India)
New Zealand
Newfoundland (see Canada's Maritime Provinces)
1936 . . . on the Continent
North Africa
Oslo (see Stockholm)
Paris
Paris (Fun in)
People's Republic of China
Portugal
Province of Quebec
Puerto Vallarta (see Mexico's Baja)
Reykjavik (see Stockholm)
Rio (Fun in)
The Riviera (Fun on)
Rome
St. Martin/St. Maarten (Fun in)
Scandinavia
Scotland
Shanghai (see Beijing)
Singapore
South America
South Pacific
Southeast Asia
Soviet Union
Spain
Spain (Great Travel Values)
Sri Lanka (see India)
Stockholm, Copenhagen, Oslo, Helsinki & Reykjavik
Sweden
Switzerland
Sydney
Tokyo
Toronto
Turkey
Vienna
Yucatán (see Cancún)
Yugoslavia

SPECIAL-INTEREST GUIDES

Bed & Breakfast Guide: North America
Royalty Watching
Selected Hotels of Europe
Selected Resorts and Hotels of the U.S.
Ski Resorts of North America
Views to Dine by around the World